POLITICALLLY INCORRECT
PARENTING
Before Your Kids Drive You Crazy

Nigel Latta

HarperCollins*Publishers*

Author's note: The names and identifying details of people mentioned in this book have been changed to preserve their privacy.

HarperCollins*Publishers*
First published in 2010
by HarperCollins*Publishers (New Zealand) Limited*
P.O. Box 1, Auckland 1140

Previously published as *Before Your Kids Drive You Crazy, Read This!* 2006
by HarperCollins*Publishers (New Zealand) Limited*
P.O. Box 1, Auckland 1140

HarperCollinsPublishers
31 View Road, Glenfield, Auckland 0627, New Zealand
25 Ryde Road, Pymble, Sydney, NSW 2073, Australia
A 53, Sector 57, Noida, UP, India
77–85 Fulham Palace Road, London W6 8JB, United Kingdom
2 Bloor Street East, 20th floor, Toronto, Ontario M4W 1A8, Canada
10 East 53rd Street, New York, NY 10022, USA

National Library of New Zealand Cataloguing-in-Publication Data

Latta, Nigel, 1967-
Politically incorrect parenting / Nigel Latta.
Previous ed. published as: Before your teenagers drive you crazy, read this!. 2008.
ISBN 978-1-86950-865-4
1. Parenting. 2. Parent and teenager. 3. Teenagers—Family relationships.
4. Adolescent psychology. I. Latta, Nigel, 1967- Before your teenagers drive
you crazy, read this! II. Title.
649.125—dc 22

Cover design by Natalie Winter
Cover photography by Alan Dove
Internal typesetting by IslandBridge
Printed by Griffin Press, Australia, on 70gsm Classic
70gsm Classic used by HarperCollins*Publishers* is a natural, recyclable product
made from wood grown in sustainable forests. The manufacturing processes
conform to the environmental regulations in the country of origin, Finland.

Contents

What the . . . ?

Right now out there in Parentland normal mums and dads like you and me are being pelted with all kinds of mad stuff. Here are just three completely barking examples:

1 Not only are there books telling you how to teach your baby sign language, but there are parents who are doing just that very thing, right at this very moment.

2 You can buy special foam crash helmets for toddlers learning to walk so they don't bump their heads.

3 There is new evidence that global warming isn't caused by rising CO_2 levels at all, but rather by rising parental guilt/anxiety levels as we're constantly assailed with new 'information' about all the stuff we're doing wrong and all the stuff that could go wrong.

My response to all this nonsense is threefold:

1 Are you kidding me? Sign language for babies? What on earth could a small incontinent person who's never been anywhere, or done anything of consequence, have to say that could be of any possible interest?

2 If your kid needs a crash helmet to learn to walk, then walking is the least of their problems.

3 In an effort to stave off parental guilt/anxiety-fuelled global warming, and thereby save the planet, I wrote this book.

I hope you enjoy it.

Preface

Never mind the kids . . . save yourself!

One could be forgiven for thinking that, somewhere between about 1982 and 1992, they started making kids from different stuff to all the previous generations of kids that had ever gone before. Up until then, kids were kids. They fell over, got dirty, played with their friends, and did all kinds of things that kids had always done. They rode in cars without triple-certified child carseats, walked to school by themselves, played in playgrounds with concrete paths, lived in houses without those little plastic plug point-guards, and ate stuff with truckloads of food colouring in it with a mad abandon.

It's a wonder the human race made it through those reckless decades at all.

Somewhere along the way, however, we all started to lose our way a bit. Life got busier and more complicated. Soon we got mobile phones, desktops and DVDs. The people who sell shampoo and the like decided that there was a thing called Generation X, who in their turn decided they didn't want to decide about anything. Now I think we're up to Generation Z, and the people selling shampoo are still trying to make soap sound like rocket science.

Soap is soap, people, let's not forget that. It isn't really honey extracts and aloe: it's soap.

In amongst all that, kids seem to have been getting steadily more complicated, and apparently more delicate as well. You could be forgiven for thinking that the poor wee bunnies were made of glass the way some people talk. Somewhere along the way some sandal-wearing hippy started calling kids 'young people', and it's all been pretty much downhill from there.

In addition, every time you turn on the television some reporter is telling you about some new research from the University of Poomfahfah which clearly demonstrates that we're all basically completely crap and our children are doomed because we're so crap.

Of course there's a 98% chance that the reporter is wrong, because in my experience journalists do an appalling job of covering social science research. In fact be wary whenever anyone is telling you what science has 'discovered' about children. I am constantly amazed — and often actually appalled — at how woefully, and sometimes wilfully, inaccurate many so-called 'experts' can be.

Beware experts.

Particularly experts who write parenting books.

As an example of how mad the world has become, let me tell you briefly about one of my own experiences as a parent. When my elder son started school he had a few speed wobbles to begin with.

He's a great wee man and I love him to bits, but he's also as stubborn as a mule that has been genetically altered and had a super-stubborn gene welded onto the toughest chromosome in the bunch. (After extensive and very complex psychological testing I have concluded he gets this from his mother.) He'd been having a few settling-in issues — testing the limits and the like — which is simply how he does business. My boy is a fence-rattler.

His teacher at the time was great — very experienced — and was on to him from the start. My wife and I breathed a sigh of relief when we first met her, because we knew she was the best first teacher we could have had for our guy. However, halfway through this meeting I suddenly tumbled to the fact that she was diplomatically asking our permission to discipline him in class when he pushed too far.

I told her that she had our full confidence and she should do whatever she thought was right. 'Put him in a box in the cupboard if you think it'll help get the message through,' I said, hoping that she knew I was joking and didn't think we actually did that at home. I also told her that, if he came home saying his teacher had been mean to him, we wouldn't be ringing her up whining about how she'd upset our little angel. We'd ask *him* what *he'd* done in the first place.

It's absolutely barking mad that teachers feel they need to ask parents' permission to discipline children at school. They do, of course, because the whiney brigade will ring the school as soon as their dear little ones get home, anxious that poor wee Tarquin's self-esteem may have been irreparably damaged.

Teachers needing to *ask* if they can discipline kids? We've *really* lost our way.

Sometimes Tarquin might actually need a metaphorical boot up the jacksie, so to speak.

Everything has become so bloody complicated. Many of the simple pleasures are being eroded away because we're so frightened, anxious, and self-doubting as parents. We're all desperately worried about screwing it up and making our children emotional cripples for life.

Here's the thing, though: we *all* screw it up in one way or another. We're parents — that's our job. Just like we have to survive them, our kids have to survive us. If they can make it past us, then they'll probably be fine. Think of it as a form of social 'natural selection'. Raising kids is the greatest form of reality television there is, just without the television. The other down side is that you can't vote people off, which is a bit of a shame. You also don't get a million dollars at the other end. You do, though — if you're half-decent and a bit lucky — get some pretty nice memories to grow old with.

Keeping pace with all this complication and preciousness has been a host of books and documentaries telling you all about how you should raise kids to minimize the chances of turning them into emotional cripples. You can buy books about how to raise the smartest kids, the most confident kids, the most creative kids, the most free-spirited kids, and every other kind of kid you could ever think of.

Bollocks to all that. This is not one of those books.

And yes, I fully get the irony of me saying this when I'm the guy who made *The Politically Incorrect Parenting Show*, and who has now also published a number of books on raising kids that (in my mum's opinion) are the best ever written. So, yes, there are buckets of irony to go around here. The problem is that if you want to get a message out to people then books and television shows are pretty much the only way to do that. I suppose I could have gone for carrier pigeons, but I don't think our cat would have coped with the stress of the endless cooing. There's no way around the fact that if you want to get a message out, then telly and books are pretty much the most cat-friendly way to do that.

However, this book is not going to be full of stuff that will just make you feel even more stressed and burdened. Raising kids is hard enough without adding more to the pile. Instead, this book is about how you can get through the first 10 years of your kids' life without going nuts. It's not easy to raise kids and stay sane, but it can be done. It *is* possible, hard as that might seem to believe. If, however, you only want to know how to raise little Tarquin and Portia so they can play Mozart on the piano-accordion at age four, then this book is probably not for you.

If, on the other hand, you want to find a way to get through the first decade without going completely mad, then this book *is* for you.

Although here's the weird thing: even though this book is about you and not how to raise a baby Mozart, you're actually more likely to raise a balanced, happy, smart kid if you're not crazy.

The crazier *you* are, the less well *they* tend to do.

The happier *you* are, the happier *they* will be.

It's a simple rule, but it's an important one. In fact, I think it's the most important rule of the whole damn lot. *You must stay sane at all costs.*

Introduction

Tricks of the trade

My job is fixing kids.

Simple really.

I work with all kinds of kids, but I especially enjoy working with the kids who end up in the too-hard basket. I like those kids — I like them a lot — and I like that basket. The little people who end up in that basket have an ability to knock the wind out of the world in a way you just can't help but admire. If you've got a 10-year-old who's defeated every expert that's ever been put in front of him, then that's a boy I'd like to meet. The kid who can make a room full of shrinks shake their heads in dismay is a kid I'd like to get to know.

As a result I've spent the last 20 years working with all kinds of kids with all kinds of problems from all over the world. I've seen them all: the rudest, the meanest, the scariest, the angriest, the saddest, and also the nicest.

There are worse jobs.

A while back I was driving home after visiting one of my families. Things with this particular family had been pretty dire at the beginning. When I first met them the eldest daughter, aged 10, had been in an in-patient ward for young people with extremely disturbed behaviour. She was admitted after she'd tried to kill herself. It wasn't a serious attempt on the face of it, but then how serious does a 10-year-old have to be? Her younger brother, still at home, was off the wall as well, throwing tantrums that were very loud, and very aggressive. Mum was a good soul but at the end of her tether. Things were falling apart.

I'd sat in a meeting some months ago whilst all the people who'd seen the girl over her stay in hospital had their say about what they thought was wrong. There were a lot of labels being thrown around — some of them pretty impressive, some less so. Truth be told, I kind of tuned out in the middle for a bit because all that stuff starts to sound the same after a while. The collective view was that it would be at least 18 months before the girl would be able to go home, possibly as long as two years.

At the end of it I waited for the plan that I was sure would follow, the way forward, the fix. There was a whole bunch of degrees in the room, and a bunch of postgraduate diplomas as well. Someone would surely come up with a plan that would fix this little girl and her family. Unfortunately that's when everyone looked at me.

Bugger.

'Hopeless cases' seem to have become my specialty. I'd like to think this is because I'm much smarter than everyone else, but sadly I know this isn't true. There are far cleverer people than me in the world; I know this because I meet them all the time. In truth I think it's because my major strength is maintaining optimism in the face of certain defeat.

I've developed an ability to look at hopelessly twisted situations and somehow figure a way out. More often than not this comes down to two crucial factors: first, having the unshakeable belief that a way out does indeed exist (especially when all the available evidence and all good common sense would suggest that it does not), and secondly, the unshakeable ability to ignore all the complicated stuff and focus on very simple things. Over the years I've met more desperate parents than I could begin to count, and more 'out-of-control' kids than you could fit in a very large and very well-fenced area. The nice thing about working a lot at this end of the scale is that you soon discover that the same principles apply across the board. You fix a 10-year-old who wants to stab his mother the same way that you fix a five-year-old who won't sit still at the table.

So this particular day, I was driving home; it was four months down the track, and things were a heap better. The girl wasn't home yet, but she was having visits at the weekends that had been going very well. In addition, her little brother's extreme behaviours had all but disappeared. They were happy again. Generally the future was looking bright; certainly a world away from that highly technical, label-heavy meeting where I'd first met the family. I hoped to have them all back together again quite soon.

All I'd done was give mum a simple yet effective behaviour management tool (a cool little thing I call The Ladder of Certain Doom, which is far more benign then the name might suggest, something I talk about later in Chapter 17), and helped them figure out some ways to get on better with each other. Relationship is everything — once you get that, you're over halfway there.

I remember driving home that day thinking about all the other families out there struggling with their own stuff. I have two kids of my own and so know first-hand that struggling with stuff really sucks. I'd seen the huge difference a few simple tools had made for this family, and thought what a shame it was there wasn't some way to work with more families, so that more people could get this simple information, not just the ones I see as part of my practice.

Then it occurred to me that there was.

In the end I wrote this book as much for me as I did for you. I have two boys, and there are many times when, despite what I do for a day job, I feel just as lost as the next parent. As an example, a few years ago one of my sons, a toddler at the time, was going through his 'Drunken Viking' stage. This was primarily evidenced by the fact that at the end of each meal he would throw his half-finished dinner plate over his shoulder and laugh as one might laugh at the end of a long night celebrating the sacking of a small island nation. He would bellow mightily as pasta and broccoli dripped from the walls.

Try as we might, nothing seemed to stop this behaviour. Each night we ended up sitting amidst the ruins of yet another heathen feast. It was actually quite damaging for my professional self-esteem because — despite the fact I spent my days telling other people how to stop their kids from running away, robbing banks, and lighting fires — I couldn't stop my own kid from throwing his plate.

How crap was I?

In the end, the only way I could figure out what to do was to stop thinking like a parent and to treat my own family like a case I was working on, a technique I use to this very day. When I'm in 'dad mode', I find the ground regularly disappears from beneath my feet. When I'm in my clinical psychologist 'fix-it mode', the way is always clear.

Love blinds us. That and fatigue.

As a result we won the battle of the dinner plate . . . only to be outsmarted when our boy promptly moved on from the 'Drunken Viking' phase to the 'Evil Criminal Genius' phase. This stage was marked by a disturbing tendency to stand halfway up the stairs and laugh maniacally, much as an evil criminal genius might do after blasting Paris with a death ray. Just as you get a handle on one stage, they move on to the next. We're always a step behind.

Which is why this book is as much for me as it is for you. I wrote the kind of book that *I* want to read. When I'm in parent mode I need something that will tell me what to do, but in a way that makes sense in the real world. It's all very well to say 'Be consistent', but have you ever actually *tried* to be consistent?

Give me a break.

As a parent I feel the craziest when I don't know what to do. These are the moments where I feel like running for the airport, grabbing the tickets and fake identity I have stashed in a locker there, and boarding the first flight to a non-extradition treaty country.

When I know what to do, everything's fine. I'm in control and life is good. When I'm lost, all I want to do is run as far and as fast as my legs, a credit card, and a Boeing 747-400 will carry me.

In the pages that follow I'm going to take you on a whistle-stop tour through some of the cases I've worked on over the past 20 years so I can show you the tricks I've learned over that time. I'm going to talk about some common problems (like sleep, toilet-training, and temper tantrums), and some less common ones as well (like baby hippos, little girls who will only eat mushy peas ice cream, and nine-year-old fascist dictators).

As well as that I'm going to take you on a visit to Harry and Sally Humdinger's house. When this Harry met that Sally the forces of chaos rejoiced. Harry and Sally have some of the most out-of-control, over-the-top kids you could ever hope to meet. The reason I'm going to take you to meet the Humdingers is so that you can see how the same principles apply even at the far end of the scale. Actually, I'm going to let you fix the Humdingers all by yourself, but we'll save them for last, once you've got all the stuff you'll need to get the job done.

All the cases in this book are real families, just by the bye, including the Humdingers, although obviously names and certain key details have been changed to protect the actual families involved. You probably won't find Harry and Sally Humdinger in the phone book under 'H', and if you do then they aren't these Humdingers.

You should always remember, too, that *all* parenting books — including this one — are just someone's opinion. I struggle with 'experts' who tell parents that unless you bring your kids up their way then your children will suffer some terrible consequence.

There are few if any issues in Parentland that are anything like that cut-and-dried. My advice when listening to advice is to always keep in mind that *you* know your kids best, and so *you* need to be the one who makes the final decision about what's best for them. I've got a few tricks and things in here I hope you'll find helpful, but the final call about what's best for your kids is down to *you*.

Now, that said, the good news about all the tricks I'm going to show you here is that they're very simple. You can do them first time out of the box without any practice at all.

Girls and boys, you most definitely *should* try this at home.

The rules

These are the rules; this stuff underpins everything I say when I'm sitting in rooms with desperate parents.

You can jump ahead and read a few of the cases first if you really must (and let's face it, just about everyone will), but once you've had a look at one — two at the most — then come back and read this stuff. It's important. Seriously.

You need all this to get the most out of the rest of the book. The things I talk about with the kids and families in the cases that follow will make a lot more sense if you understand the principles that run the whole thing.

1

Ten simple rules for raising kids

Every time I sit down with a new family, there are a number of simple principles I follow to keep me on track. The way can get a little confusing sometimes — most times in fact — so you need a few signposts to keep you headed in the right direction.

As a parent, you need to have rules as well, not just for the little people, but for the big ones too. If you don't have some broad principles to follow, then chances are you're going to get lost somewhere along the way. Principles are good. Principles are the things you hang on to when the fog rolls in. Principles will get you through any situation you come across because they tell you which way is up.

After working with thousands of kids, and raising two of my own, these are the ones I think are most important. There are 10 of them in all, and while there isn't going to be a test on this stuff at the end, you might want to keep them handy at least for the next 15 to 20 years till your kids leave home. The good thing is that they'll never become obsolete or need upgrading.

All you need to do is keep them somewhere handy in your head and you'll get through just about anything.

1
Remember the three Rs

Relationship, relationship, relationship.

This is the most important one of them all. If you remember nothing else, you have to get this one cemented firmly in your head. Relationship is all you ever have. People who forget this are heading for a pile of hurt. It's easy to control kids — fear will do that pretty adequately. The problem is that they get bigger, and eventually they stop being afraid. At that point the tables are usually turned fairly rapidly.

If fear is all you have, then you are in *big* trouble. Take it from me, because I've seen the families where parents thought that simply frightening kids into being good was the best way to do things, and they are not happy people. In fact, these are some of the unhappiest families I ever see.

Discipline is *all* about relationship.

Everything I talk about in this book is underpinned by the belief that the relationship you build with your kids determines both how they will behave, and who they will become. The most important job you have as a parent is to build strong relationships with your kids. If you just focus on that alone, then you'll probably be OK 98.6% of the time.

2
Loving is easy, liking is hard

Most kids feel loved by their parents, even the ones whose parents beat and abandon them. Kids pretty much *assume* love. The same cannot be said for feeling liked. The great majority of kids I see don't feel *liked* very much at all. In fact, most of them are convinced their parents don't like them at all. The reason for this is that the great majority of parents I see really are struggling to like their kids. By the time they get to me, stress and frustration are piled up layer on layer till they can hardly feel the ground any more. 'I love him, but I don't like him very much anymore' is something I hear a lot.

Kids need to feel *liked*. Loving is almost automatic, but there's a clear choice in liking. Liking is something you do because you want to, not because you have to. Loving is about duty. Liking is about fun, about play, about the best stuff.

The expression of the quality of the relationships which contain the family can most easily be seen in the extent to which playfulness is present in the house. Playfulness is the grease of family life — it is the stuff which keeps the wheels turning. Without it, things inevitably grind to a painful halt. Whenever I sit with families and see an absence of playfulness, I start to worry.

If discipline is all about relationship, then it is equally true that relationship cannot exist in the absence of playfulness. One can love amidst the blackest of emotions, but playfulness requires a little light. Don't worry, though. I'll show you some ways to get there if that seems a little daunting at this point.

3
Children are piranhas

Children are attention-piranhas. They are ravenous. They can devour a cow-load of attention in one sitting. They are so hungry for this stuff that they go into a feeding frenzy whenever there's some to be had. They are so hungry for it that they'll do anything to get it, even if this means doing things that ultimately are self-destructive. Your average child-piranha will swim right out of the river and up on to the bank chasing a cow-sized dose of attention, even though this means certain destruction. You have to understand this, because if you don't, you won't feed them enough. This is not a good strategy, because if you don't feed them enough, then they'll turn on *you*. Children, like piranhas, are hungry for attention, and they live only to feed.

Hungry piranhas are naughty piranhas, and you definitely do not want hungry, naughty piranhas in your home. Keep them well-fed and they'll stay in the river where they belong.

4
Feed the good, starve the bad

Following on from the whole piranha-thing is this one: You have to be careful about *what* you're feeding. This is all very simple and obvious, but kids can make you so crazy you neglect the simple and obvious things because you're so busy trying not to go insane. You have to remember to feed the good stuff and starve the bad.

If you feed something, it will grow. If you starve it, then it will fade away. This is very simple, but most people having problems with their kids have lost sight of this, or they haven't stopped and had a good long look at what they're feeding.

Good behaviours should be fed lavish dollops of attention and praise. Bad behaviours should get the coldest of shoulders.

If you feed the bad behaviours with your attention, you will grow monsters.

As we go on, I'll show you more about what this means in a practical day-to-day sense, but just for now implant this one firmly in your brain: feed the good stuff, starve the bad.

5
Kids need fences

If you don't build fences for your kids, you're an idiot. This might seem a bit harsh, but how does one kindly point out to an idiot that they're an idiot? As with anything, though, there are subclasses of idiocy.

Hippies, for instance, don't build fences. Hippies think kids should be free to roam the world. Groovy, baby. Lazy People don't build fences either. Lazy People think it's easier to do nothing. Uh-huh.

Anxious Nellies also don't build fences. Anxious Nellies don't want to restrict poor wee Tarquin and risk damaging his fragile little self-esteem. If you're a rolling-of-the-eyes kind of person, this would be the time to do it.

Gumboots don't build fences either, because they want to be *friends* with their children. Gumboots want to be pals, not parents.

All of these people end up in my room: the Hippies, the Lazy People, the Anxious Nellies, and the Gumboots. All of them unhappy, and all of them wondering why their child is such a horror.

Kids need fences. Make rules, set limits, and stick to them as hard as you can. It is in the nature of children to move forward until they come up against a fence. Some kids need only to know that the fence is there, others need to bang into it several times, but *all* of them need it.

A world without fences is a dangerous and frightening place for a little person. Fences say 'You can go this far, but no further.' Fences keep you safe and secure. Fences help you figure out where your place is. Fences keep out the bad stuff as well.

Let me say it again: *kids need fences*.

6
Be consistent-ish

When I was first starting out as an idealistic young clinical psychology student, things seemed so much clearer and easier. I'd sit in rooms with tired, desperate parents, and wonder how they couldn't see the problem. It just seemed so blindingly obvious to me.

'The secret,' I would tell those poor people with all the Zen-wisdom that a 20-something, childless, trainee-shrink can muster, 'is that you have to be *consistent.*'

I would say it just like that, labouring the last word as Moses might have done when he brought his load of wisdom down from the Mount. Sometimes you need a bit of careful emphasis to ensure the masses grasp the profundity of what you're saying. Moses and I both understood that.

Be consistent. So obvious.

What a complete bloody idiot I was. Well-intentioned for sure, good-hearted I would hope, but an idiot just the same.

Somewhere along the way I had children of my own — two boys — and then *everything* changed. Now my definition of consistency is that if I can *consistently* avoid the all-too-frequent impulse to throw the kids out the window, it is a good day.

Everything else is up for grabs. Everything. Even consistency. *Especially* consistency.

When you're a parent many of your decisions are made on the basis of whatever is going to make you feel the least crazy. If I went for help with my kids and ended up seeing the 20-something version of me, I'd slap him silly. Absolutely ear-ringingly silly.

'*Consistency?*' I'd shriek in a high-pitched, slightly hysterical voice as I merrily slapped away at him while he tried to crawl under a chair, squealing like a baby. 'That's brilliant,' I'd say, reinforcing the point with another backhand. 'Why didn't *I* think of that, you clever, *clever* man.' I'd slap him till my hand was stinging, and feel extraordinarily good about it.

So be as consistent as you can.

Strive for absolute consistency if you must, but just don't be too hard on yourself when some days you come up a little short on the consistency stakes.

7

Don't take any crap

I am constantly amazed at the amount of crap some people will tolerate from their children. I've watched seven-year-old boys say the most utterly disrespectful things to their parents and I'm the only one in the room who seems bothered by it. Some wee madam mouths off at her mother and her parents sit there as if nothing has happened.

Hello?

That stuff is *not* going to happen in my room. If that wee madam or wee man says disrespectful things to their mum or dad in my room, then the first thing that happens is I jump on it. Then once the kids are out of the room, I jump on all the big people sitting around ignoring what just happened.

You can't always stop kids from dishing out the odd bit of crap. That is the nature of all children from time to time, but you don't have to take it. You don't sit there and let it go. If you do, then you're headed for trouble.

You don't have to be a cruel dictator who squashes any signs of dissent.

Dissent is a natural part of the process. Disrespect, on the other hand, is a whole other thing. Dissent and debate are good. They're signs that you're doing your job — signs that your kids are growing up and developing minds of their own. You want them to have a mind of their own because, by the time they're ready to leave home, yours will be worn out and in need of a rest. They're going to need minds of their own — trust me — so dissent is a good thing.

Disrespect is not a good thing. It is, in technical terms, a crappy thing.

And you must not take it.

8
You must, must, must have a plan

The only things that happen by accident are accidents. You don't want to parent by accident. I've seen parenting by accident and it isn't pretty. You want to parent by design, which means you must, must, must have a plan.

Now, by this I don't mean that you have to sit down and do some kind of nauseating new-age business-plan-type exercise. You don't need to write a 12-page document setting out your achievable goals and measurable outcomes. You don't need to go on a retreat once a year and engage in an evaluation of the previous year's plan (unless of course you want to use that as an excuse to ditch the kids on the grandparents for the weekend while you take off somewhere nice for a couple of days).

So relax. I'm not advocating any of that silly nonsense. However, you do need a plan.

What I mean by this is that, from time to time, you need to sit down and figure out what the hell you're going to do *before it happens*. If you're having problems, then you have to take a bit of time to work out exactly what the problem is, what your options are, and then decide what you're going to do to fix it. You don't need to take a long time to do this. Sometimes a single ad break might be enough, sometimes it might take a little longer. Whatever the case, you do need to take the time to stop, and think, and plan.

Throughout the rest of the book I'm going to show you exactly what I mean by this, because we'll look at lots of different plans that I made with lots of different families struggling with lots of different problems. For now though, just at the general level, remember that you must always have a plan.

Look before you leap, baby — that's all I'm saying.

9

All behaviour is communication

This one is simple, but incredibly important.

When I look at the behaviour of any kid, regardless of who they are, or what they're doing, I always start from the premise that the behaviour is the little person's way of saying something they either can't or won't say in words.

Behaviour is simply another form of communication. Climbing out a window and running off into the night is simply a way of telling people stuff. Children are far more likely to use behaviour to communicate than they are to use words. Usually this is because they don't have that many words. They do have a lot of feelings, but they usually aren't very good at using words to convey those feelings.

As a result they tend to *say* how they feel by *doing*.

Bad behaviour is not just bad behaviour — it is the little person's way of having a conversation. Usually it means that one of the previous eight rules are being neglected in some way. Bad behaviour is usually the little piranhas' way of getting attention. They are hungry, and so they feed as best they can.

My job with the kids I work with, and your job with your own kids, is to figure out what their behaviour is saying. What do they really want? Most times if you can work out what the behaviour really means, then you're 75% of the way to fixing it.

10

Embrace chaos

Recently I was talking with a friend about how much our lives had changed since we'd had kids. He made the comment that he loved hearing busy professional types talk about having children

— doctors and lawyers and the like — and the way a lot of them believed it was possible to have kids and still get everything done. It's easy, they say, you just have to schedule your way through. You just have to get organized.

My, how we laughed.

When you have kids, you invite the forces of chaos into your life. You can no more schedule your way through the madness of raising kids than you can schedule your way through a tornado. When the wind blows, you go.

Understanding and accepting this is important. If you don't, then you'll fight the chaos. You'll rail against the injustice of it all. You will think that it should be easier, and this will make you feel resentful, bitter even.

Embrace the chaos with a cool Zen-like calm because it is mad for us all.

Some nights in our house, for no apparent reason, things just go completely barking mad. The planets simply align in the wrong way and all hell breaks loose. This very night for instance, only three hours earlier, we were in the middle of several minor eruptions. The little people were grumpy, then naughty, then resistant, then it all just plain imploded. It was like a scene from one of those end-of-the-world mini-series. People were running and screaming everywhere.

At such times, all you can do is go to your quiet place, and ride the storm all the way through to the end. There's no point fighting it, because there is no way to escape the madness of such moments. All you can do is keep your hands on the wheel, keep your eyes on the compass, and ride the storm till the seas calm.

As I write, a warm cup of coffee wafts at me from the desk, the boys are tucked up in bed sleeping like recently fallen angels, and their mother is snoozing in front of the telly. All is right with the world. In eight hours they'll all wake up again and we'll set sail once more, but just for now life is sweet.

Embrace chaos, Grasshopper. What choice do you have?

The rules

1 Remember the three Rs.

2 Loving is easy, liking is hard.

3 Children are piranhas.

4 Feed the good, starve the bad.

5 Kids need fences.

6 Be consistent-ish.

7 Don't take any crap.

8 You must, must, must have a plan.

9 All behaviour is communication.

10 Embrace chaos.

2

If you read only one chapter, make it this one

There's a reason this chapter comes in at number two, and that's primarily because it's one of the most important bits of the whole book. It is, in fact, the over-arching philosophy which informs almost every plan I've ever come up with to help struggling parents. The 10 principles in the previous chapter are important, but this one is so important that it gets its own chapter. It's deceptively simple, and so a lot of the time people skip right past it without taking the time to really take it in and get to grips with it.

Don't be one of those people. Take a moment, Grasshopper. Rest your racing mind and free yourself of your everyday material concerns. I'm going to give you the *real* Golden Rule, and — make no mistake — this puppy is 24-carat pure bling. If you can really *get* this one, you're going to find that almost every aspect of parenting will be considerably easier.

Ready?

OK, here it is: *don't make their problem your problem.*

Surely it can't be that simple? I hear you say.

Actually, I think it is.

To understand that, though, you need to think like an economist. Up until a few years ago I used to think that economics was what people who worked in banks were interested in. I thought economics was simply all about foreign exchange rates and inflationary pressures. To my great surprise, I've since discovered that economics is just as relevant to raising kids as it is to raising interest rates.

Why?

Because every day our children plot and plan corporate takeovers in their very own financial system. They are ruthless traders in the naughty economy, and like all Wall Street types they want to take over the world. They bargain hard for the best deal they can get with little concern for anyone but their shareholders.

The naughty economy

A very simple economic principle drives behaviour in children — and in all of us in fact — and it's this: how much does it cost? Before you decide to do something, you have to decide if the cost of the behavior is worth the outcome. For example, if you're three years old and you want to throw a block at the cat, you need to weigh up the costs and benefits of the behaviour.

On the plus side it's kind of fun to throw stuff at the cat, because it's intensely interesting to explore what sort of effect blocks have on cats. Also the cat generally bolts out of the room, which, if you're a three-year-old megalomaniac is very satisfying indeed.

Finally, this type of behaviour gets them some quality one-on-one time with Mum and/or Dad, who then explain that we don't throw blocks at Fluffy.

On the downside they might get put in their room, or the blocks might be taken away.

So before they throw, they need to decide if the benefits outweigh any potential costs.

Simple economics.

So why is the golden rule so golden?

The reason for the glittery goldenness of the golden rule is that it focuses you on tipping the balance of the cost–benefit analysis in your favour. It's quite simple really, because if you make it *your* problem then they won't really care. If you make it *their* problem, then they will. If the cost to them of being naughty is small, they'll keep being naughty. If the cost to them outweighs any benefits from being naughty, they'll stop.

The problem with the modern economics of good behaviour

All this flies a little in the face of 'modern' thinking about managing children's behaviour, which is all about giving loads and loads of praise and rewards for good behaviour. In this 'child-centred' view, the idea is that we essentially make the rewards for good behaviour so strong that they'll automatically choose to be good.

So what could possibly be wrong with that?

Well, in my experience I think it overlooks the fact that being naughty is ferociously good fun. It just *is*. Being good is great, and ticks on star charts and pats on the head are all fine and well, but there is something utterly compelling about being naughty. I don't see this as a bad thing; it's just the way we are. If we were all naturally good, then we wouldn't need the police and prisons. The bitter truth about us *Homo sapiens* is that being naughty is a powerful reinforcer all by itself. Being nice to your little sister is great, but pushing her over is also pretty cool when you're three and a control freak. Eating dinner nicely is fine, but throwing the plate across the room when you're bored is also hilariously funny. Similarly, staying in bed at night is perfectly reasonable, but nowhere near as enticing as the thought of running down the hall shrieking at the top of your lungs. You can poop in the toilet if you want the pat on the head, but dropping a big log on the living-room floor is far more entertaining.

The truth is that praise and rewards will only get you so far with children. Ultimately, they will all be drawn to the dark side of the force from time to time. They will want the thrill and power that comes from bucking against the system. The only way to stop that stuff in its tracks, in my experience, is to make the cost of doing it far outweigh any benefits.

The key warning sign you need to put the golden rule to work

This one is so simple it's astounding. Basically, if you're dealing with any kind of behavioural issue — be it naughtiness, whining, not staying in bed, sibling conflict or whatever — the rule of thumb is that if you're feeling more wound-up about it than they are, you need to shift the balance back onto them. If you're feeling more angry/stressed/wound-up about behaviour at the table than they are, then the system is out of balance. If you're telling them off and they're acting like they don't care — or worse that the whole thing is a big laugh — then you need to shift the balance back onto them.

Ask yourself this question: Whose problem is this right now — theirs or mine? If the answer comes back that it's yours, then it's time to act.

How to do that

Obviously I'm going to cover all this in a lot more detail in the chapters which follow, but for now — and in case this really is the only chapter you read from the whole book — let me give you the cut-down bare basics.

The thing to understand is that the golden rule ('don't make their problem your problem') is like a grand principle. It's a rule you apply whenever you and your little one disagree over what should be happening. In this light it isn't a specific technique *per se*, but an attitude, an approach. What this means is that you have to change what you do so that the consequences for what they are doing are bigger for them. You simply have to increase the cost of the bad behaviour until it becomes so expensive that they can't afford it anymore.

Let me give you a few examples to show you what I mean in a very practical way.

❖ If little Timmy laughs when he's in time out and comes out acting as if he doesn't care, then simply leave him in there longer until the boredom wears out all his cheeky good humour.

❖ If Jane keeps getting out of bed at bedtime and running into the lounge and driving you crazy when you're trying to watch telly, then put her in her wee room and lock the door until she gets the point that if you come out of your room, it's going to cost you a bit of isolation.

❖ If Mary won't eat her greens, it costs her her dessert.

❖ If Max can't play nicely, it costs him increasing amounts of time sitting by himself.

So the next time you find yourself frustrated, flummoxed, and generally confused about what to do next, ask yourself: Whose problem is this? If the answer is that it's yours, all you need to do is shift the balance so that the cost of what they're doing becomes so expensive they simply can't afford to keep doing it. You might be surprised how much this simple focusing of thought can shift the commanding heights of the naughty economy in your home.

Keep this one in mind as you read through the rest of this book, assuming of course that you do read through the rest of the book.

Inside little people's heads

One could be forgiven for thinking there probably isn't much going on inside a little person's head — the box being so small and all — but actually the reverse is true. In a bizarre twist of biology, there is far more inside your children's heads than there is in yours and mine.

Over the past 25 or so years, we've learned an amazing amount about what happens to children's brains as they grow, and how this has an impact on their thinking and behaviour. We also know a great deal about how our interactions with children shape the very structure of their brain.

In this section we look at three different aspects of the little mind: first, some of the incredible things we've learned about brain development in children; second, some simple but effective communication tools to make your job easier; and finally, how you can encourage your children to use the equipment contained in that head a little better. I'll also tell you the *real* secret to making smart babies: the more you understand about what goes on inside little people's heads, the better you'll be able to function in yours.

3

The 'little' brain

A brain may look like a big wrinkly grey walnut, but that's where the nut comparisons end, because the brain can do things the humble walnut couldn't even begin to imagine. Even the mighty cashew — surely the most splendid of all nuts — is no match for the human brain.

Having said this, it is probably true that nuts taste better.

In the past, we've had to rely on animal studies and people who have had bits of their brains damaged, destroyed, or sometimes even had small pieces fall out. Now we have machines that can help us look deep inside the workings of the brain without having to leave the comfort of our seats or, perhaps most importantly, having to have bits of people's heads fall out. Magnetic Resonance Imaging (MRI) and Positron Emission Tomography (PET scans) aren't just things Dr Carter yells on: they're actually real tools neuroscientists use to study how brains work.

As a result we've learned some truly amazing things about how brains develop, and the impact of both our genes and our environment on that process. For instance, it used to be that we thought that brain development depends on the genes you inherited from your parents, with the environment having only a limited impact. Now we know the truth is far more complex. In reality, brain development is hugely impacted by the interplay between genes and environment. Our interaction with both the world in general and specifically the people looking after us affects the very architecture of the brain.

Just a quick warning

I'm painfully conscious of the fact that there's nothing which can raise parents' anxiety levels more than talking about kids and brains. Just the merest mention of this stuff can set parental pulses racing as we instantly slip into semi-panic mode worrying that we've either done too much of the bad stuff or not enough of the good stuff, thereby damning our precious little ones to a lifetime of stupidity and ugliness.

The good news is that you can relax, because it isn't quite that simple. I'm going to go into this in more detail below, but for now just keep in mind that if you're the kind of parent who reads parenting books, then you will almost certainly already be doing all the important stuff.

A brief user's guide to the brain

The brain itself, whilst often seen as a single organ, is perhaps more accurately a collection of closely related systems. In the deeper layers of the brain are systems which regulate core body functions, such as thirst, hunger, heart rate, and breathing. Interestingly, the centres of the brain that mediate our emotions are also amongst the most primitive areas of the brain. Higher functioning, such as spatial organization, language, and reasoning, is managed in the cortex, which is the outermost wrinkly bit.

The basic building block of the brain is the brain cell, or neuron. The brain of a foetus has approximately twice as many neurons as it will need, undoubtedly on the basis that it's always good to have a few in reserve. Most are shed *in utero*, and an average newborn baby's brain is composed of approximately 100 billion of these highly specialized cells.

Neurons are connected by tiny 'branches' called axons (of which there is usually only one per cell and which *send* signals) and smaller hair-like projections called dendrites (which are numerous and *receive* signals from other neurons). This jumble of axons and dendrites is analogous to the brain's wiring. Electrical impulses pass through the axons and stimulate the dendrites of surrounding brain cells, which in turn pass the message on.

At birth, a great many of the 100 billion neurons are still not connected, and it is one of the key tasks of the developing brain to form and reinforce these connections. In the first 10 years of life the brain forms literally trillions of these connections between cells. A single neuron may connect with up to 15,000 other neurons in an incredibly elaborate network of dendrites and axons. By the time children are two years old, the number of connections has reached the same levels as in adults; by age three, their brains have approximately 1000 trillion connections, which is about twice that of adults. The cortex of a newborn is largely dormant, but by the age of one the cortex is highly developed.

So what happens to all this extra brain power?

Life.

Throughout life the brain engages in a process of growth and elimination. Over time, as the child experiences different things, some pathways are strengthened and some are discarded. Repeated stimulation of a particular pathway strengthens the connections in that part of the brain. Lack of stimulation causes the connections to effectively die off. All of which means that the phrase 'Use it or lose it' is particularly apt.

Interestingly, humans come into the world with brains that are the least developed of all the primates. Macaque monkeys, for instance, are born with a brain that looks a lot more like their adult brain. Humans are the only primates in which the brain continues to grow at the rate it did in the womb for at least two years before even starting to slow down. Indeed the fatty myelin sheath — the brain's equivalent to the plastic insulation around the outside of the axon 'wiring' — isn't fully formed until age six.

All this means that humans are the most sensitive of all the primates to environmental influences. The environment shapes our brains far more than it does any of the other hairier monkeys. Somewhere in the order of 75% of human brain development happens outside of the womb and is directly affected by the immediate environment.

The secret to making smart children

You might think that the best way to make your kids really smart is to get all the flashcards, the Baby Mozart DVDs, the educational toys, and teaching them their times tables at age three, and all that other malarkey.

It isn't.

If you really want smart kids, then don't make babies with stupid people. It's as simple as that. If you want smart babies, make babies with the smartest people you can find. Our genes play a pretty big role in how smart we are, so if you make babies with a significant other who is a bit of a thicky, then you're starting from the back of the field IQ-wise. Unfortunately, if you didn't think about this and have already made babies with a stupid person, this will come as a bit of a blow, so you're best to try to optimize things as best you can. Oddly enough, all the educational toys still probably won't make much difference. In reality, what you're best to do is make your home a place where your kids receive what we in the trade call 'warm, consistent care'.

So what's all that about then?

The importance of warm, consistent care

If you think about the fact that little brains come into the world super-primed for learning — through the active formation of these connections between neurons — and that over the first few years of life the little person's experiences effectively 'hardwire' in actual structural changes to the brain — by way of these connections being either strengthened or discarded — then the importance of the early years becomes much clearer. Young children are essentially building a physical representation of the world inside their heads. Their brains are trying to wire in ways of responding to the world that they will then use to steer their behaviour for years to come.

If the message which is constantly being reinforced is one of chronic distress or fear, then the brain of the child will effectively hardwire this in, and thus reflect a 'stress structure' all the way down through life. For example, children who have been chronically traumatized during the first three years of life have been shown to have a higher resting pulse rate than that of normal children. Indeed, the chemicals produced by stress have been shown to effectively kill off brain connections, which explains why many children with this background experience significant delays in tasks such as language and reading.

Luckily for those of us who don't subject our kids to chronic trauma, the converse is also true. Studies have shown that children who experience warm, consistent care (bearing in mind my earlier comments in Chapter 1 about being consistent-ish) hardwire in a set of connections that will prepare them well for the trials that life brings. These children tend to respond better to stress both in terms of their physical reaction (producing lower levels of stress hormones) and their behaviour. They are likely to do better in school and to develop strong social skills. They are given higher teacher ratings, and are generally more robust and successful socially and academically.

It is this combination of consistency and warmth that is key. Kids don't need flashcards and endless repetition of their times tables at age three. They need parents who are attuned to their physical and emotional needs, and who are consistently meeting those needs. In this way, the little person's developing brain forms an abundance of connections that help them negotiate their way through whatever problems life may bring.

If you are connection-rich, then you have more options on a number of fronts: you are better able to understand and manage your feelings, to make friends, to deal with defeats, and to learn in school.

The way that you become connection-rich is to have parents who are warm and consistent. Forget the flashcards, and focus on keeping things rolling along in as even a way as time and patience allow. Just as importantly, try to have a bit of fun from time to time as well.

Growing little brains

There are a number of important implications from all the research on brain development for parents. The important thing with all this is not to get too wound up and neurotic about it. If you raise your voice from time to time, you won't damage their little brains. If you scream all of the time, then you probably will. Below are some of the broad recommendations that the neuroscience boffins make for everyday mums and dads like you and me:

❖ Provide kids with good nutrition, maintain their health, and provide a safe environment. All fairly obvious really. If you want to build a healthy working brain, you can't do that so well on sugar and chips. There's nothing wrong with a bit of junk food, but all children do best on a healthy and nutritious diet.

❖ Develop a warm, caring and consistent relationship with your children. Actively work to make them feel safe and secure. Their relationship with you is the foundation on which they build their own life, and results in a connection-rich brain.

♣ Learn to recognize your child's individual needs and respond to them. Read their behaviour and moods and try to react accordingly. Play when they want to play, and then teach them how to sooth themselves when they need to calm down.

♣ Talk with your kids, and read and sing to them. Language is hugely important, and the way children develop their language skills is primarily through interaction with you.

♣ Encourage them to play and explore the world, including the worlds of other children. The more they can get out and experience life, the better. Similarly, the more they are with other children, the more they are able to develop their relationship-building skills.

♣ Provide routines and discipline, because these foster a sense of security and safety in children. Like I said before, kids need fences.

♣ Become involved in your children's education. This doesn't mean you become a nutty obsessive parent and pump them to learn to spell by age two, but it does mean you show an interest. Get involved, talk about the things they are learning, and encourage and support their curiosity and interests.

♣ Above all, don't go crazy. If you are stressed, tired, or not coping, your interactions with your children will be affected. In the rest of the book I'm going to look at ways you can deal with many of the behaviours that drive parents nuts, and also ways to establish much happier relationships with your kids.

There's an awful lot of research that tells us our job as parents is a very important one. Not only do we shape their behaviour, we also shape the actual wiring in their little brains. Just remember, though — like I said before, don't get all panicky and anal about this stuff. Tuck it away somewhere and do the best that you can.

We *all* shout.

We *all* say unkind things from time to time.

You won't turn them into brain-damaged emotional cripples by raising your voice or losing your rag from time to time. Just make sure that the majority of the time you're tuned in to their little minds, and as nice as you can be.

Simple, really.

4

Talking *with* little brains

If you want to avoid stomach ulcers, high blood pressure, and premature death, then you have to learn to talk *with* your children. I can put it no more bluntly than that. We all talk *at* them from time to time (and on bad days we may actually shout stuff at them), but talking *with* kids is the key to a longer, healthier, less crazy life for you all.

There are lots of reasons why it's good for children to have parents who are receptive and responsive communicators, and we've talked about much of this in the preceding chapter. Little brains organize their very structure around the stuff to which they are exposed. This is all fine and well, but what we haven't talked about yet is why it's good for *you*.

Simply put, communication, or the lack of it, lies at the heart of most conflicts within families. I've sat in rooms with people who can shout at each other for hours and still no one manages to hear anything except the sound of their own voice. If you can't communicate properly with your kids, you're setting yourself up for years of conflict.

And if you think kids behave badly when they're little, wait until they hit their teens — if the bedrock upon which the family rests is fractured by years of conflict, then you're headed for hard times. I've seen those families close up, and that is not a good place to be. Adolescence can be hard enough to survive, what with all the perfectly normal craziness, without further compounding it with years of crap communication.

One of the most important skills kids need to learn is how to deal with their thoughts and feelings. They have a lot of both, and if you don't teach children how to process and deal with their thoughts and feelings, then it will almost certainly come back to bite you, and it will definitely bite them.

So heed my words, because this *truly* is battlefield wisdom: if you want to be sane at the end of all this, you have to build a good communication platform with the little people in your house. If you don't, then you're setting yourself up for years of stress, tension, worry and guilt. The law of the jungle might be 'Eat or be eaten', but the law of families is *communicate* or be beaten.

Sometimes, though, they will bore you witless

It can make you feel like a bad parent to admit that sometimes you find your children boring — but, trust me, you aren't alone. I love both me dear sweet little lads to pieces, but there are times when they're talking about things that are so utterly boring that I almost want to poke myself in the eye. The reason for that is that their worlds are so much smaller than our worlds. They haven't really done much, or seen much, and so they can sometimes fixate and obsess over things which seem . . . well . . . mind-numbingly trivial.

As an example, we had to ban talking about SpongeBob in our house at one stage, simply because my wife and I became so utterly sick of SpongeBob stories that we had no choice. Don't get me wrong, I love the little yellow square guy, and am a big fan of the show, but it just isn't that funny when a six-year-old is recounting a scene, badly, for the 227th time.

Similarly, Lego Bionicles: while they are a very cool toy, they have become the bane of my life. My youngest son has talked about Bionicles so much, and in such intricate detail, that he has pushed many words I need for my day-to-day professional life out of my head to make space. Just the other day I was on the phone to a lawyer and I couldn't remember the word 'complete'. It was gone — completely and utterly gone. Oddly, I could have told this very same lawyer all about the history of conflict between the Bionicle tribes of the Glatorians and the Skralls, including the names of many of the subtribes of the opposing sides . . . but I couldn't remember the word 'complete'. So now Bionicle talk is severely restricted, purely because I'm terribly afraid that unless I put a stop to it now there will be no useful words left in my head.

That you get bored with your kids from time to time isn't bad, it's normal. When you get bored, it's fine to simply tell them you need a break and that they should go off and play.

'But Dadda,' my youngest son protested after I had said just this to him after several minutes of non-stop Bionicle genealogy, 'aren't you happy that I know so much about the Bionicles?'

'Sure I am,' I said. 'But it's enough for me to know that you know. I don't have to know what you know, just knowing that you know it is all I need to know to know that I'm happy. Any knowing past that initial knowing is more than I need to know. You know?'

He frowned. 'What?'

'Go and play, dearest monkey boy.'

Happily for us both, he did.

Power-listening

OK, let's be honest: there is no such thing as power-listening. That's just something I made up to increase the chances of you reading this bit. If I'd called it 'listening', you probably would've skipped right past because you'd think you already knew it all. You call something power-listening and people get a bit more interested.

Like I said in the previous section, no one expects you to listen to your children 100% of the time. This is simply not possible, because they talk so much and a fair percentage of it is weird, or simply mind-numbingly trivial. It is deeply fascinating to them, to be sure, but sometimes it can be less so for the big people. Despite the best of intentions, you will find yourself tuning out from time to time, nodding vacantly and going 'Hmmm . . . yes . . . good . . . OK . . . right . . .'

Anyone who says they *always* listen to *everything* their children say is either a big fat liar or a big fat crazy person, or worse still a big fat lying crazy person.

You need to be careful, however, because as the kids get older they may be asking permission to do something you wouldn't actually want them to do.

> 'Jimmy, where's your little sister?'
> 'I traded her to my friend Mathew for a skateboard.'
> 'What? Why in God's name did you do a crazy thing like that?'
> 'You said I could.'
> 'No, I didn't.'
> 'Yes, you did. I asked you if it was OK and you said "Hmmm . . . yes . . . good . . . OK . . . right . . ." Don't you remember?'

Listening to children is more than just not talking. Even very little people know the difference between someone who is listening and someone who is simply not talking. Listening is important because it helps you to understand what is going on for the little person, but just as importantly it gives them the message that what they are saying is interesting and important. Listening encourages talking.

There are some simple tricks you can use to help you listen to your kids more effectively:

Give them your full attention . . .

Make eye contact and focus on what they are saying.

Sound interested . . .

Tone of voice is important, because your tone must match the words you're using. Saying 'That's very interesting' in a bored tone doesn't work.

Be animated . . .

Kids love over-the-top gestures, and facial expressions help your kids feel appreciated and also enjoy talking with you. Try it and watch their faces light up.

Ask lots of questions . . .

The good thing about questions is they signal interest and engagement. As a general rule, kids like it when you ask them questions. The best questions to encourage discussion are the open kind that require more than a yes/no answer: 'What did you do at school today?' versus 'Did you have a good day at school today?'

Reflect . . .

This doesn't mean just repeating back what they've said, but also reflecting back in words the feelings they are talking about as well. Be a mirror for your little person so they can see themselves through your eyes.

Praise their ability to explain things . . .

It's very important to let your children know you actually enjoy listening to them, and also that they're good at explaining things. If they feel confident in their ability to talk about their thoughts and feelings, they will try and do this more.

Clearly you won't be able to do all this stuff all the time, and you probably shouldn't, because if you do then you'll either die of exhaustion or go crazy, or both. You don't have to listen *all* the time, but you do have to listen *some* of the time. The nice thing about children is that the apparently trivial stuff they burden us with now — SpongeBob, Bionicle genealogy, *High School Musical* trivia — is a practice run for the much bigger issues which wait somewhere up ahead on the track. In my experience it's always best to practise when the stakes are lower, so that when you get to the important stuff you've got a well-practised ear.

Figure out how they see the world

We all have different ways of seeing the world and of interacting with those around us. There is simply too much going on to invent new rules for every single situation, so instead our brain organizes itself into templates, kind of like a mental map of the world, and it uses these to decide how to respond to new situations. Essentially, we develop this mental map to help navigate through the infinite number of choices we are faced with every day. Maps are a way to bring some semblance of predictability into what is essentially an unpredictable world.

Having said this, it's important to understand that the map is only a representation of the world, and not the world itself. It is subject to biases or perspectives that are derived from our previous experiences. If your experience as a child is that no one listens to you when you're upset, this will have a huge impact on the relationships you develop over the course of your life. As we've seen in the previous chapter children begin building maps almost from the moment of conception, and continue this process throughout their lives.

Our job as parents is to make sure that our children are using maps that are as helpful as can be. If you've ever found yourself wondering why your child *always* seems to do this, or *never* seems to do that, the answer is probably because of the map they're using. Some kids will almost always take the easy road, and some the hard road. Some kids seem determined to find out for themselves about every last thing, and others are too timid to leave their parent's side. All of them are guided in their decisions about what to do by the maps they carry in their heads.

There are two main ways you'll be able to get some idea about the maps your kids are using. The first is by listening to how your children talk about the world, and the second is by watching what they do.

Children give you clues about their maps all the time when they talk. If you listen carefully, you'll hear them:

* ♣ *Why do I never get to go first?*
* ♣ *Why are you always angry?*
* ♣ *No one ever wants to play my games.*
* ♣ *I like sharing.*
* ♣ *My friends are fun.*
* ♣ *I'm good at reading.*
* ♣ *I hate reading.*
* ♣ *My teacher is mean.*
* ♣ *My teacher is nice because she helps me.*
* ♣ *That's not fair.*
* ♣ *No I can't come. I have to finish this first.*
* ♣ *That's not nice.*

All of these statements tell you things about how the little person making them sees the world. They all contain assumptions about the world and how it works; some are positive, and some not so positive. When you listen to your children, pay particular attention to anything which sounds as if it could be a rule: for example, statements which contain the words *always* and *never*.

Similarly, listen for the things they like and dislike about other people: for example, *My teacher is nice because she helps me*. This suggests a map which says that helping people is nice. Of more concern would be this statement about the same teacher: *I hate my teacher because she always says I get things wrong*. This implies that the child has a rule that help is bad.

Basically, you listen for statements which sound as if they are being driven by some kind of belief or value, and might be used to guide decision-making. The statement *No one ever wants to play with me* is clearly driven by a map of the self as being undesirable, and could lead to the child withdrawing from others because their behaviour is driven by the underlying negative map.

The other way you'll see glimpses of your little one's mental map is simply to watch them. When my oldest son was about eight months old, I watched him try to climb some stairs. He was single-minded in his pursuit of the summit. He wanted no assistance of any kind. He *was* going to climb the stairs, and he was going to do it *all by himself*. I remember thinking this was the first time I'd really seen a clear glimpse of who this little gurgling man really was. He possesses that same approach to life still. In his case, this single-minded determination is both a blessing, and a curse. There will be a lot of good that comes from such a strong focus, but there will also be a cost. My job is to help him edit the map he's developed so he can find the best way to wherever it is he decides he wants to go in life.

If you watch your children, you will see how they do things, and indirectly the rules that they use:

❖ when they play with toys

❖ when they draw pictures

❖ when they play with friends

❖ when they attempt to solve problems

❖ when they try a new task

✤ when they go into strange situations
✤ when they succeed and when they fail.

All of these things will tell you how your little one goes about the business of life, and indirectly the map they're using to make their choices. For example, if every time your child is presented with a new task they freeze up, this tells you things about the map they have which determines their confidence in themselves. This child thinks it's better not to try than to fail. Similarly, if whenever they fail they burst into tears and are inconsolable, this tells you things about how they perceive defeat.

The good news is that little people's maps are far more malleable than big people's maps. Little people's maps tend to be drawn more in pencil than in indelible ink. This means that if you notice a rule that you think will not be helpful to them (*No one likes me* or *It's better not to try than to risk failure*) you can intervene and help them to redraw the map.

You can't help your kids be happy and successful in their lives — however you choose to define success — if you don't know how they see the world. None of us likes to have other people's views of the world foisted upon us. That doesn't work with adults, and it doesn't work with children either. If you felt bad and someone told you 'Well, that's ridiculous — just feel better', that probably wouldn't work. It would probably only succeed in annoying you. Little people are the same. If you understand how they see the world, then you can help them find an easier way through the world. You have to start from where they are, and work it out from there. In the following chapter, I'm going show you how to do that.

5

Rewiring little brains

Children with extreme behaviour problems are frequently referred to me. In a given day, I could be working with a 10-year-old who smears faeces and kicks holes in the wall whenever he's told off, then a 14-year-old gang member whose one ambition in life is to stab someone, then an 11-year-old girl who has chosen not to speak to anyone, ever, and then a nine-year-old boy who periodically has to be restrained by the police when he has a major 'tantrum' because people are worried he might seriously injure either himself or someone else.

On the face of it, these are all complex kids with a bunch of stuff going on. It's easy when faced with that level of complexity to become a bit lost. Because of this, I've always taken a very simple approach to solving problems. Essentially, I see all problem behavioural issues as a deficit in one of three areas:

♣ a deficit in skills (don't know what to do and/or how to do it)

♣ a deficit in ability (the step is too big)

♣ a deficit in motivation (don't care enough about it to want to do it).

As a result, when I sit down with a kid to try to figure out what to do, I'm looking at those three areas: skills, ability, and motivation. I want to know if the step I'm asking the child to take is simply too big, whether they have the skills to take that step in the first place, and if there is sufficient motivation to take the step. Once I have a clear picture of what the child's current functioning is, then I work backwards from the goal. This means you take the behaviour you want (such as healthy expression of anger), break it down into steps, then simply teach each of those steps to the child, focusing on their particular pattern of deficits. Essentially, you help them fill in the gaps.

The same approach can be used for your own children. Often I see families where children are struggling with issues their parents don't know how to help them with. Some of the common ones include:

✤ anger

✤ low self-esteem

✤ shyness

✤ lack of confidence

✤ trouble making and/or keeping friends.

The problem with problems is that often our emotional reaction to the difficulties our kids are facing stops us from getting a clear picture of what's actually happening. Often when I ask parents to describe the specific behaviours they're concerned about, they have some difficulty doing this. Many parents can tell me that Johnny or Jenny gets very angry, but it is often difficult for them to describe the specific steps Johnny or Jenny takes to get angry.

The trick in helping children overcome problems is to break it all down into specific steps, and use that as your guide for getting to the happy ending. As the saying goes: you must, must, must have a plan. For example, 'shyness' is a rather broad term that encompasses a range of specific behaviours. Many parents struggle to help children who are shy, and often feel at a loss to know what to do. In the following example, I'm going to show you how you can use my simple three-stage model to help your child deal with shyness:

1 describe the problem

2 identify gaps in either ability, skills, or motivation

3 fill in the gaps.

Whilst we're talking here about kids who struggle with being shy, it's worth remembering that these steps can be used with almost any problem you might face. Below, I take each stage in turn and talk about how it applies to the problem of 'shyness'.

Stage 1: Describe the problem

➤ Describe the behaviours of concern
With new children she sits or stands nearby, playing by herself quietly, constantly glancing over towards the other children.

➤ Describe the steps taken to get there
Sees unfamiliar children, becomes quiet, fidgety, and anxious, stands for a couple of minutes thinking, decides to withdraw, goes to edge of group, begins to play by herself, keeps looking back at group as she plays.

➤ Describe any exceptions
When with her cousin will join in playing with other children. Begins first playing with her cousin alongside the new children, and then within a couple of minutes starts to talk/play directly with the other children.

➤ Identify strengths/weaknesses
Her major weakness is in the initial stages whereby she has trouble getting over the hump of physically entering the group. Her major strength is that once she has joined in she can relax and play normally.

It is important to identify any exceptions to the behaviour, because this can highlight some very important strengths that might otherwise have gone unnoticed.

Stage 2: Identify gaps in ability, skills, or motivation

Once the problem has been clearly defined, we move on to the second stage, where you identify whatever gaps your child might have in ability, skills, or motivation that might be preventing them from reaching the goal.

➤ Identify the shared goal (remember that it has to be something you both want)
Self-directed joining-in play with new children.

➤ Break this down into steps
Having contact with new children.
Figuring out what the children are doing.
Making the decision to join in the game.
Positive self talk: 'Other kids will want to play with me'.
Physically approaching the group.
Asking if can join in using confident voice.
Joining in with the group activity.

➤ Apply the information about your child's strengths/weaknesses to identify where their gaps are (ability, skills, or motivation)
Her major gaps are probably at the stage of making the decision to join in, the positive self-talk, and the physical approach to the group.

Stage 3: Fill in the gaps

Now you're ready for the third and final stage where you 'fill in the gaps'. This means you help your child to develop the specific skills they need to get there. A key issue for many parents is often *how* to teach their child a new skill, particularly if it's something like 'making the decision to join in' as in the example above.

Many parents have some idea what to do — they just have no idea how to do it. For this reason I have listed below a number of very simple techniques, in no particular order, that you can use to help kids master a new skill:

➤ Externalize the problem

Instead of talking about the problem as if there's something wrong with the child (he's shy or she's angry), you make the problem some fantasy creature that is external to the child ('the jinglies' for anxiety, or 'the angry monster' for anger). Rather than saying 'You just have to stop being angry', you say 'You have to beat the angry monster'. Rather than saying 'Don't be shy', you say 'Let's see if you can beat the jinglies this time'. The idea is to work together to beat the angry monster, rather than the child feeling bad that they can't stop being angry.

➤ Model the skill

Take your child to a place where there are lots of kids, like a playground. Watch the other children playing, and pick out some who are modelling the target skill and talk about how they must have done it.

You can also model it directly yourself. Pick a relevant situation and then go do the thing yourself. Afterwards, explain to them how you did it. Then do it again and ask them if they saw how you did it that time.

➤ Use teaching stories

Stories are wonderful teaching devices. At bedtime, instead of reading a story book, make up a story about the little girl who couldn't speak to children, or the little boy who was troubled by an angry monster. If you aren't good at making up stories go to the library and look for relevant stories. They do exist — you just have to look.

➤ Solve someone else's problem

Have a conversation with your child about this other kid you know who has a problem, and then talk with your child about how the other kid can solve their problem. For example: 'I once knew a kid who found it hard to ask people if she could play with them. What do you think she could do to get better at that?'

➤ Practise the skill in play
Children learn vast amounts through play. Join in and direct the play so that the toys are faced with the same challenge your child is, then have your child act out a number of solutions.

➤ Praise
It's obvious at one level, but sometimes we forget the basics. Any movement in the right direction should be praised immediately and lavishly. Praise is to children as sunshine is to plants. If the sun shines, they grow. There are more specifics about praise on page 170.

➤ Don't lecture them; ask how they will solve the problem
Everyone switches off from a lecture. No one likes it. Little people are just the same. Instead of telling them what to do, ask them how they will solve the problem. Teaching children how to think is a fundamentally important part of parenting and a very useful tool.

If you use these simple steps, you should be able to deal with a great many of the common difficulties of childhood. Many of the common concerns parents have can be managed in this way. The old chestnut of kids having 'low self-esteem' can be more easily managed when you specify what that actually means, work out your child's current strengths and weaknesses, identify your goal, break that down into bite-sized steps, and then tick off each one as you go. If nothing else, you at least have a plan to begin with instead of feeling as if you don't know where or how to start.

Sleep

Let's start with the easy stuff. Sleep problems, despite the extreme stress they can cause parents, are usually pretty straightforward to fix.

This might seem like an infuriatingly glib thing for me to say if you've been struggling with sleep problems in your house, but it's true: sleep problems are very easy to fix.

The amount of time it takes can range from 10 minutes to a week or so, but rest assured that the fix is there to be had.

I'm going to show you three families with sleep problems, with kids ranging from little babies up to eight-year-olds, and difficulties ranging from molehills to mountains, and the simple things you can do to fix things up in a jiffy with kids of different ages.

6

The baby who slept for 10,000 kilometres

NEW REFERRAL	
Family details	Shane (29) and Mandy (28), and newborn son Connor (5 months)
Presenting problem	Connor will not settle to sleep, apparently ever! Parents up all night in shifts. Mandy says they are both going insane from sleep deprivation. Sounds desperate on the phone.
Notes	Shane is a truck driver, so fatigue a bit of an issue.

You don't need a degree to spot parents with kids who aren't sleeping. There is a special kind of haggard 'look' that develops around them, much as certain trees attract certain kinds of moulds. Exhausted parents live under a furry grey coating so thick you can almost touch it.

You expect to be tired when you're a parent of a young child. You prepare yourself for it, and to a large extent it's unavoidable. You will lose sleep. If you're lucky, you'll lose a little — if not, you'll lose a lot.

Shane and Mandy looked like the walking dead. They looked like extras from a zombie movie. At first I thought they might have been middle-aged Goths because of the dark eye make-up. Then I realized it was not eyeliner but exhaustion that had carved out the deep bruised hollows under their eyes. They looked so tired I didn't know whether to offer them a coffee or call an ambulance.

'Come in,' I said, hoping I wouldn't have to physically carry them into the room.

'He just never sleeps,' Mandy said after they'd collapsed into their chairs.

'Never?' I asked, although, to be honest, from the look of them I was fully prepared to believe that Connor had come out wide awake and had stayed that way ever since.

'Well, he sleeps a bit,' Mandy continued, 'but it doesn't ever seem to last for more than two hours.'

'Tell me about your night-time routine,' I asked.

Mandy looked at me numbly. Shane just sat there — his eyes were open, but it was hard to tell if he was even breathing. Shane might have just died in my office.

'You know,' I said, 'night-time. The bit when the sun goes down.'

'We . . . umm . . . we don't really have one, specifically I mean,' Mandy said.

Things were bad for these poor people. The line between day and night had started to blur so much it was getting hard to tell them apart. 'Can I get you guys a coffee?' I asked, deciding that chemical stimulants were the key to any further progress.

Shane stirred, not dead yet apparently, which was a tremendous relief: 'That'd be great thanks, mate.'

After the coffees, things picked up a little. It turned out that Connor had been a dream for the first two weeks of his life, as many little babies are. He'd slept almost all the time he wasn't feeding. Just as they were both starting to really feel as if they had the whole parenting thing licked, little Connor woke up. From that point on, their lives had become a misery. The only way they could get him to sleep was to put him in a front pack and walk him around the house. And here was where the real nightmare had begun, because that was the *only* way they could get him to sleep. Since that time they had walked him constantly all hours of the night and day. They took it in shifts, much as sherpas might take it in turns to carry the heavy stuff up mountains.

'We must have walked 10,000 kilometres in the last five months,' Shane said, briefly roused from his coma by the excessively strong coffee I'd made him. 'Every time we stop and put him down he starts to cry.'

'What do you do then?' I asked, already knowing the answer.

'Pick him up again,' said Shane.

'Have you ever tried leaving him?'

'A few times,' Mandy said.

'And what happened?'

'He just kept crying and crying.'

'And so you picked him up again?' I asked her.

She nodded. 'Yes.'

'OK,' I said. 'Let's get some stuff sorted so this little guy can get a decent sleep and you can both start to feel something approaching normal again.'

They nodded eagerly, although I could tell that the stimulant effect of the caffeine was already beginning to dull. Soon they would return to their undead state. We had to work quickly.

Where things went pear-shaped

Sleep is a skill we must learn. Much as it would be nice to think so, sleep doesn't come naturally. Sleep, or rather the ability to settle oneself into sleep, is something you have to *teach* your kids. The other side of this particular coin is that little babies are the fastest learners around. They come out with hungry little brains that are desperately trying to make sense of this big buzzing confusion. Babies' brains want rules to understand the world, and if you're not careful they'll start to make up their own.

In Connor's case, he'd done just that. In the absence of a sensible structure from his mum and dad, he'd made up the rule that sleep only happens whilst being strapped to your parent's body and being walked. This was only marginally manageable at five months — it certainly wasn't going to work as a long-term solution. They weren't going to be able to carry him when he was 15, spotty, and listening to crap music.

In truth, if they didn't get some sleep soon Mandy would probably be a widow because Shane would drive his truck into something one day. This would be a great weight of guilt for poor old Connor to grow up with, being responsible for his father's death and all, so I decided it was best to simply fix the sleep problems and save all that money and time Connor would have to spend on counselling later in life to deal with his unresolved guilt issues.

Baby-whispering for idiots

Remember from Chapter 1: *all behaviour is communication*. When babies cry it is their way of signalling to the world that all is not right in Eden. One of the most important things you have to do is figure out what is going on, meet the particular need, and get your little one off to sleep.

Now, there are people who have written whole books on baby crying and what each individual little snort and whistle means. I absolutely believe it is possible for someone to be able to tell a huge amount from the particular wails, grunts, and gurgles coming from babies. If they can do it for chimpanzees and hippos, why not for little people? Unfortunately, because I haven't devoted my life to the understanding of baby communication, it's all a bit of a mystery to me. I learned what most of the shrieks from my own kids meant over time, but I'm lost with other people's kids. Crying to me often just sounds piercing and irritating.

So in lieu of complicated descriptions of the taxonomy of baby crying, let me give you the cut-down idiot's guide. Basically, there are five main things little babies are trying to tell us when they cry:

- ♣ 'I'm hungry.'

- ♣ 'I've got wind.'

- ♣ 'Oh heck, I just filled my pants with evil-smelling waste products.'

- ♣ 'I don't feel well.'

- ♣ 'I'm overtired.'

Just as I did with my boys, you will learn (or probably already have learned, or are simply past the whole thing and are already blocking it out of your memory) how your precious little person signals their various brands of displeasure. Obviously you run through this list each time.

- ♣ Have we fed the child today?

- ♣ Does the child have windy-pops?

- ♣ Are the nappies in a poor state?

- ♣ Is the child sick?

- ♣ Failing all that, is this just a wee person who is so tired that they are now almost hysterical?

The first four issues are fairly easily addressed. The last one is the subject-matter that we'll turn to next. Before we do, though, let me just say that you need to trust your instincts above all other things. If there is something about the crying that sounds different, or not right, or you just plain have a funny feeling about it, then go to a doctor straight away. Parents with children live at the local after-hours medical centre; if nothing else, if a doctor has looked at your child and said there's nothing up, then at least you can be reassured when you're doing the things that I'm going to talk about next.

The importance of warm-down

First off, all children, no matter how old they are, need a bedtime routine. They need cues to understand that the time has shifted from 'awake time' to 'sleep time'. This is all pretty bloody obvious, right? Except of course to many people it isn't, or at least they simply don't understand the importance of warm-up — or warm-down in this case.

The purpose of the routine is to provide the baby with a set of cues to help them begin to prepare for sleep. If the baby learns the steps into sleep time, then they will be more prepared to settle when they get to the cot. The cot should not be a surprise.

A good evening routine is fairly simple to establish. I recommend the following:

1 Dinner (not too late or it will all start turning to custard half way through — the kids, that is, not the dinner).

2 Bath time (bubbles, fun, splashing, etc).

3 Stories for the older ones.

4 Off to bed in a familiar, comfortable surrounding where they feel safe and secure.

5 They then go to sleep.

6 Big-people time (this is the bit where you have a couple of hours to watch telly, have a cup of tea, and pretend you still have a life).

Night-time routines are important. If you get that right, then you'll have good sleepers right the way through. If you get it wrong, as Shane and Mandy did with Connor, you'd better have a lot of patience and even more coffee. Shane and Mandy were on the road to sleep-deprived madness, and believe me, that is not a place you want to go.

When you're entering the heart of sleep territory (which is everything in the post-bathtime phase), always remember that your only goal is to be settling your little people towards sleep. Your one objective is to render the children unconscious in as short a time as possible. For this reason, what you play with them, how you play with them, what you say and how you say it, should all be focused on that one crucial objective: sleep.

This also means you need to learn to recognize the signs that your baby is tired. This can include yawning, jerky movements, becoming grumbly, and just simply looking tired. You want to get them on the cusp of tiredness, because if they go too far they'll become overtired and be even harder to settle. There is a definite window. Learn to spot it, and act when the window is open.

In the field of clinical hypnosis there is a nice phrase: 'Use a voice that is consistent with your purpose.' What this means is that, if you want people to feel light, sound light. If you want people to feel relaxed, sound relaxed. What that suggests for the rest of us is that, if you want kids to sleep, then don't shriek like a fishwife or bellow like a boilerman. Use a voice that is consistent with your purpose.

The 'crying-never-hurt-anyone' sleep programme

Crying never hurt anyone. It's true. OK, it might be possible that a person could be so busy crying that they walk out onto the road without looking, are almost hit by a bus but are then miraculously pushed out of the way by a heroic passer-by, only to fall down an open drain and get eaten by a freakishly large mutant albino alligator living in the toxic waste filled sewer. You could try and make the argument that crying killed this person, but I think all of us would agree that it was the alligator that was responsible. In any case it would be hard to argue that crying was the real problem here.

I know that there is a very vocal group of parenting enthusiasts who believe it actually *is* very bad for children to cry. I regularly get emails from some of them in fact. Often these people will quote the 'attached parenting research' and explain very seriously the 'damaging effect of cortisol on the developing brain'. They will say that crying babies show elevated levels of the 'stress hormone' cortisol and that this can have far-ranging effects on the growing brain.

All of which sounds a bit scary really, doesn't it?

Well, like most times when people start using 'science' to justify their position, you'll find that almost all of these people have sourced their 'science' from the internet and haven't read the actual science directly themselves. Instead, they're relying on someone else's reading of the science posted on some bulletin board, or they've read a book written by other like-minded people who have themselves selectively interpreted the science to back up their argument.

I'm not going to go into a long discourse on the science of crying and children here — I'll save that for another time — but let me just say this: I *have* read the science directly myself, the *actual* science in *actual* scientific journals. My unreserved view after reading all of it is that crying, in and of itself, never hurt anyone. Children are undeniably hurt from chronic neglect — such as the children raised in the horrific conditions of the Romanian orphanages, where babies were left in cots with no human interaction at all — but that's not what we're talking about here. Neglect very clearly hurts children, but a few tears at bedtime are not quite on a par with growing up in a Romanian orphanage.

In fact I believe this so conclusively that, as you'll see below, I used these very same techniques on my own children.

If you have a bad sleeper, you have to prepare yourself for a bit of crying. There isn't much of a way around this. If you find crying hard to listen to (and let's face it, most of us find it hard to hear our little blossoms unhappy), you either have to harden up or buy some industrial-grade earmuffs. There is no way around the fact that the road to good sleep is paved with tears.

All sleep programmes work on the same basic principle: crying never hurt anyone. Essentially, you leave them to cry and they go to sleep eventually. This can be hard, very hard, but it's a heck of a lot harder to go without sleep for years. Some people call this a 'controlled crying technique'. Gut-wrenching is what it feels like for many parents. The only thing you can do is dig in, stick with the programme, and don't give in at any cost.

Here's how it works:

1 Go through the normal bedtime routine as described above.

2 Settle your wee one down into bed with much quiet cooing, soothing murmurs and the like.

3 Quietly retreat.

4 When the crying starts (and it will), wait five minutes before you go back.

5 When you do go back into the room, do not make eye contact or talk. Simply pat or rock them until things settle, then exit again.

6 Wait for six minutes after the crying starts before you go back in.

7 Repeat the cycle, gradually increasing the time between visits until sleep ensues.

8 Collapse into a chair, emotionally exhausted, and worry about

whether or not your child will grow up feeling unloved and neglected, then refer back to this page and read step 9.

9 No, they won't.

We had sleep problems with our oldest boy when he was a baby. Despite having told other people how to establish good sleep patterns for years before we had children, I found myself walking around with my wee guy in a front pack at 10.30 one night — I had become the very thing I had warned other people about for years. Fortunately, when I realized this I knew exactly what to do: the crying-never-hurt-anyone sleep programme.

Except, of course, that whilst it is easy in theory to tell parents to leave their crying child, it's bloody hard in practice to do it with your own kid. My wife and I did the programme, but it was certainly gut-wrenching. We sat in our living room one afternoon listening to our wee man scream, and it was horrible.

'Are you sure this isn't hurting him?' my wife asked me, looking as distraught as I felt.

'Well, that's what I've been telling people for years' was all I could muster.

We sat there a bit longer, listening to him scream. I was sweating. I racked my brain, going over everything I knew about children and bonding and neglect. Doubts whirled around inside me as the wailing continued unabated.

I went back in when we'd got to the seven-minute mark and he looked almost purple. Suddenly the whole crying-never-hurt-anyone thing didn't seem so certain. It actually looked as if my boy was about to explode from crying. His heartfelt shrieks sounded like the wailings of a poor wee soul who feels abandoned and betrayed. In that moment I was convinced that if he didn't explode he would be psychologically maimed. If this didn't stop soon, I was convinced he would be scarred forever.

I couldn't believe I'd been telling people to do this for years. It was inhumane, outrageous. It was cruel and unusual punishment. It was obviously the worst thing you could ever do to a child. I came back out of his bedroom. My wife was sitting with her head in her hands. The baby was about to explode, and it was all my fault.

'What are you doing?' she asked, watching me pick up the phone.

'I'm calling Mum.'

Amazing really. Three degrees, a postgraduate qualification in clinical psychology, and 10 years' experience working with some of the most difficult kids you could imagine, and my response was to call my mum. Do we ever *really* grow up?

'Hi, Mum.'

'Hello, dear, how's it going?'

'Not so good — we're doing a sleep programme.'

She laughed. 'Is that him in the background?'

'Yeah.'

I could almost hear her nodding. 'It's hard sometimes.'

'Look,' I said, business-like as the bands of stress tightened around my head 'Did you ever leave us to cry?'

'Of course. I had four kids, I couldn't rush in all the time.'

'How long would have been the longest you left me to cry for before I went to sleep?'

She thought for a moment. 'Probably half an hour or so.'

'Maybe longer sometimes?'

'Could have been. You were a bit of a stubborn boy at times.'

I made a quick mental note to edit this bit out when I told my wife. I also felt a tremendous sense of relief. Already I could feel the stress lifting. 'And I don't hate you, right?'

She laughed. 'I'd like to think that was true.'

'It's true,' I said. 'I don't hate you at all. I haven't been scarred by the experience one little bit.' I smiled, feeling a steely resolve set in. 'Right then, his little goose is cooked.' In that moment I knew I could stick with the programme. I'd been left to cry and

I didn't hate my mother. My little guy wasn't going to guilt me into giving up. 'Thanks, Ma,' I said.

When I got off the phone I told my wife what my mother had said.

'And you don't hate her?'

I shook my head confidently. 'Nope.'

We followed through with the programme, and even though it was hard for a bit (it took us about a week) we got there. We went from bad sleep to excellent sleeping in a few days. To this day he is still a great sleeper, as is his little brother. And best of all, they show no outward signs of hating us.

'You're so lucky your boys are good sleepers,' people have often said.

No bloody way.

Luck had nothing to do with it.

Fixing Connor

I went through the sleep programme with Mandy and Shane. They looked a bit uncertain, so I told them the story of my telephone call with my mother, which seemed to help.

I rang them the next day. 'How'd it go, Mandy?'

'It didn't work.'

'Why not?'

'He just wouldn't stop crying.'

'What's the longest you left him for?'

She paused a bit; a guilty pause. 'Five minutes.'

I smiled, having been there myself. 'And then what did you do?'

'Picked him up.'

'And?'

'And he went to sleep straight away.'

'You know what I'm going to say, don't you?'

'Yes.'

'I don't hate my mum, Mandy, and my kids don't hate me.'

'OK.'

'You know what to do, right?'

'Right.'

'I'm going to ring you back at the end of the week, OK?'

'OK.'

'Be hard.'

'I will.'

Friday morning, I rang up again. 'Well,' I asked, 'what news?'

Mandy sounded brighter. 'It's a miracle.'

'What? He walked on water?'

She laughed. 'Better than that. He slept through from 7.30 last night until 6.00 this morning.'

'Amazing,' I said.

'It was incredible,' she said. 'A whole night.'

'Well done. What was the longest he cried for?'

'We got up to 20 minutes then he just went to sleep. Next night it was five minutes, then he didn't cry at all. He just went down, cooed a bit, then went to sleep.'

'Fantastic, Mandy — you did it!'

'It was wonderful having an evening to ourselves and then a whole night's sleep.'

'And does Connor hate you?'

She laughed again. 'I don't think so.'

'This is good,' I said. 'Now all you have to do is teach him to balance a cheque book, cook, and drive a car, and he'll be ready to get his own flat.'

'We might just enjoy sleeping for a bit.'

'Good idea. You call me if there are any hiccups, OK?'

'OK.'

But there never were.

Secrets of sleeping babies

Have a fixed bedtime routine.

Check they are fed, clean, and healthy.

Leave them to cry for five minutes then go back in and pat, then six minutes then pat, then seven minutes, and so on until they sleep.

If you get worried, check nappies and check temperatures.

Tough it out and don't give in.

If you are really worried and crying doesn't stop, then take your wee one to a doctor.

After you've done that, and reassured yourself that baby is healthy, start again.

Remember, too, that sleep programmes go out the window when children are sick.

When good sleep patterns are cemented in place, sit back and enjoy it.

7

The Soft and Gentle Sleep Programme:

not in a bed, not in my room, not with some juice, not with a spoon

NEW REFERRAL	
Family details	Mark (29) and Sarah (28), and their daughter Sam (4)
Presenting problem	They have terrible trouble settling Sam at night. She refuses to sleep in her bed and is up until very late making a huge fuss each night.
Notes	Apparently she also has a thing for spoons.

Sam was four years old. She had an aversion to beds and sleeping, and a passion for cranberry juice and teaspoons. Sam was a sparkly wee thing who bounced around the room like a little blonde bubble. To the casual passer-by she appeared cute as a button, but I could tell that after a while all the bouncing and teaspoons would start to grind you down.

So it was with Mark and Sarah. They were obviously good

74

people. Mark was an accountant and Sarah worked part-time in a law firm. They looked like the kind of people who wouldn't have just bought the parenting books before Sam was born; they looked like the sort who'd have actually read them. More than that, I bet if I looked through those books I'd find sections highlighted and pages duly marked. These guys looked like they took the business of parenting very seriously. God help them.

'She's a bit of a handful,' Mark said, as Sam played with some blocks in the corner, 'but she's pretty good most of the time.'

'Except for nights,' Sarah broke in.

'Yes,' said Mark. 'Nights are not very good.'

'Nights are horrible,' said Sarah.

'What usually happens at night-time?' I asked.

Sarah rolled her eyes. 'She won't settle, no matter what we do.'

'OK,' I said, 'paint me a picture.'

So they did. Most nights the fun started about 8.00 p.m. They waited until Sam looked like she was starting to get tired and then brought out the pyjamas. That was the first fight. At this point there was general running away and non-compliance. 'Sam, come here *now*' was the order of the day.

After the pyjama fight had been fought (which usually took until 8.30-ish), they would carry Sam upstairs to bed. She would be plopped in bed with the obligatory bottle of cranberry juice, her favourite teaspoon, and a video playing on the television in her room. Sam also liked the light on. Mark usually sat there for about 20 minutes, until she was engrossed in the television, and then he would quietly slip out.

'Most nights I get as far as the end of the hall when it starts,' he said.

'D-a-a-a-a-a-a-a-a-ad.'

'And what do you do then?'

'I go back in.'

'I see. Keep going.'

Mark would settle her and then slip out again. The next phase began when Sam would leave her room and go down the hall. Mark would return her to her bed, but Sam would be up again after a short while. This continued for hours until Sam eventually fell into an exhausted sleep, on the floor, sometime around 11.00 or midnight.

They had started leaving her on the floor with a blanket covering her, because when they lifted her up she would wake up and the whole thing would start again. Even then it didn't stop, because Sam would be up two or three times during the night, and most nights she would end up sleeping in their bed some time around 4.00 a.m.

'And what do you do when she gets into bed with you?' I asked.

Sarah sighed. 'We give in and let her stay. I know we shouldn't, but it's just easier than having a big stink at four in the morning. By then all we want to do is sleep.'

It constantly amazes me that toddlers are so adept at out-foxing and outplaying their parents. If parenting was a reality television show, the toddlers would always be the last ones left on the island. They'd be the ones who get the million dollars. Sarah and Mark had about four degrees between them, but they were being bested by a four-year-old who hadn't even graduated from preschool. (I never get too scathing about this, having been bested by my own toddlers from time to time as well.)

'Tell me about the teaspoons,' I said.

Mark laughed. 'She has this thing for teaspoons.'

'Any teaspoons?'

'Well, yes, but she likes shiny flatter ones best.'

I looked over at wee Sam, and sure enough there was a shiny teaspoon clutched tightly in one hand. 'Hey, Sam . . .'

She looked up.

'That's a cool spoon you have there. Can I see?'

She held it up, a shy wee four-year-old smile on her face, as if she were showing off the Oscar she'd just won for best visual effects in a motion picture.

'Wow. Hey, you should plant it and see if you can grow a spoon tree. Then you could have lovely fresh spoons every day.'

She looked at me in that way little kids do when they're not sure if you're having them on. My belief is that it is every adult's duty to tell outrageous lies to children. Apart from the fact that it's just plain good fun, it also makes their world a magical weird place for a while until they grow up and boring old reality sets in for the long haul.

'The only thing you have to watch out for is spoon monkeys.'

She frowned, looking quizzical.

'It's true — if you have a spoon tree, then pretty soon you'll have a bunch of spoon monkeys showing up wanting to take the spoons back to Spoon Monkey Mountain.'

'Why?' she asked.

I looked at her as if it were obvious: 'How else would they eat their custard?'

She thought for a minute and then said, 'Oh . . . yeah.' She turned back to her blocks, accepting the whole thing. Lying to little kids is good for everyone's soul.

'So tell me about the spoons,' I said to Sarah and Mark.

It turned out that Sam tended to obsess over the spoons. She always had to have one, especially at bedtime. The problem was that she kept dropping it and losing it, necessitating much turning on of lights and searching under beds and blankets until the missing spoon was found and order restored. Most nights there would be at least one full-scale search in the wee small hours.

'OK,' I finally said. 'I think I have it all now. Tell me what you want.'

'A good night's sleep,' Sarah said.

This time I smiled. 'Well, let's do that then.'

Where things went pear-shaped

Sleep with older kids is just the same as sleep with little kids. The only difference is that as kids get older they can add in ever more interesting layers of cunning and weirdness to try to win the game. Little babies are limited — pretty much all they can do is cry — but as they grow, they learn, and as they learn they get better and better at driving us crazy. Don't blame them, it's their job.

And of course they have us over a barrel, because in some mysterious little-kid way they sense that we desperately want them to go to sleep. Cunningly, they use our desperation to win the game.

Remember: all children are piranhas. They string us along with the ever-present promise of settling, and somehow manage to convey the impression that if we just do this one more thing, then they will finally go to sleep:

> *If you just get me one last toy car . . . If you just get me one last drink of water . . . straighten that curtain . . . kiss dolly goodnight . . . get me one last drink of water . . . open the curtains . . . read me one more story . . . get me one last drink of water. . . dance a wee jig with your hair painted green . . . sign this contract acknowledging that I am actually the boss of everything . . . get one last drink of water, then I absolutely positively promise I will go to sleep, I swear . . . just bring it in my Buzzy Bee cup . . . shaken, not stirred . . . OK? . . . Huh? Huh? Huh?*

Yeah, right.

They will no more go to sleep than Hitler was going to stop at Poland.

Just Poland, OK guys?

Yeah, right.

Sam was a little blonde-haired piranha with a thing for spoons. She had developed a slick routine that kept her parents dancing a jig every night. Sam would sleep, of that I was sure, but the cycle she'd created had to be broken first. Her parents had let their desperation to get her settled make them give in little by little until their evenings had become a three-ring circus.

The three Rs of sleep for little kids

Is it any surprise? Routine, routine, routine.

Routine is everything. You have to signal to kids that the time for sleeping is upon us. You have to create a warm-down, exactly as you do with little babies, that says it is now time to go to sleep. You have to get rid of anything that goes counter to this.

❖ Fruit juice is not consistent with warming down to sleep (as well as being incredibly bad for kids' teeth last thing at night).

❖ Television is not consistent with warming down for sleep.

❖ Having the light on is not consistent with warming down for sleep.

If you are having problems getting kids settled at night-time, the first thing you have to do is stop and take a close look at your bedtime routine.

Remember: you must, must, must have a plan. Have an objective look at what you do as you are warming the kids down to sleep. You need to *stop* doing anything that seems to be going in the *opposite* direction of winding down to sleep. Children will not settle unless they have a good solid routine under them.

Pilots generally try to avoid landing planes with the landing gear up, so why would you want to try to land kids without doing the same? If you don't check that the gear is down when you're on the final approach, chances are it's all going to end in lots of screeching and flames. In Sam's case we had to get rid of the juice, the television, the light, and even the spoons. We also had to get her back in bed and sleeping rather than performing. We had to get rid of the lunatic routine that Sam had engineered, and substitute it with something more sensible that the adults had developed.

Sleep Voodoo

The very last bit is of course crucial. Landing the plane is not just about having the structure underneath you; landing a plane is about technique. If you have a wee one of this age who does the in-and-out-of-bed thing, then you need to have a good finishing technique. All the routines in the world won't save you if you mess up the last bit.

With little babies, you need inner strength (or failing that, those industrial-grade earmuffs I mentioned earlier). With older kids, you need Sleep Voodoo. This is very important, so let me explain.

Let's assume you've gone through your whole routine, that all the bathing and stories and warming down has been done. At the point where the head hits the pillow, you need to change gears again, and become absolutely focused on the big goal: sleep.

When you put your wee one into bed, you have a cuddle, a kiss goodnight, and then *tell* them that it's time to sleep now. *Never* ask: 'OK, honey, can you go to sleep now?' Ask this, and what do you think they're going to say? *'Sure, Pop. I'm a four-year-old — and therefore a complete lunatic — but, this aside, I can see the merits of your request.'*

Yeah, right.

Don't ask: tell!

This doesn't mean that you become a drill sergeant, or a shrieking fishwife. Just as with little babies, you must use a voice that is consistent with your purpose. There is no place for screeching, harshness, barking, nagging, whining, or any of those things. This is the place for a quiet, warm, but very clear instruction: 'OK, honey, goodnight. It's time to go to sleep now.'

This precise moment is also the point where Sleep Voodoo kicks in. Sleep Voodoo, simply put, is the process of magically creating sleep through the process of unquestioning faith. At this point your whole being is completely committed to the fact that *sleep will now happen.* You do not entertain any doubt about this — you call it down into you as a certainty. Sleep is the *only* possible outcome.

If you doubt it or lose your faith, they will know it and sleep will not come. You must commit absolutely to the fact that sleep *will* now enter the room. Having made the decision to commit, you must now hang in there until sleep comes.

The Soft and Gentle (but slower) Sleep Programme

This is the soft and gentle way of establishing good sleep habits. It takes quite a bit longer then the SAS Sleep Programme, which we'll talk about in the next chapter, but it works. This one is great if you have boundless patience and don't like tears.

After telling yourself, the universe, and your little one that sleep will now happen, and committing yourself fully to that single outcome, you withdraw from any interaction that pulls your wee one from the sleep road. There is no further conversation, no further eye contact, no further stimulation. Depending on the degree of difficulty you have been having, you either sit very still at the foot of the bed facing away, sit on the floor or on a chair, or stand in the doorway facing away, or out of sight in the corridor. You are there, but you are not there.

At this point you ignore. You do not react. You are like a Buddhist monk in meditation. There may be screeching, and whining. There may be tears or pleas, but you do not engage. You simply accept that grumbling is part of the moment, and you do not react. You sit there, looking away, and wait for sleep to come.

As they settle, you quietly edge your way towards the door. This may take some time.

If your wee one climbs out of bed, you simply place them back in bed, without making eye contact, and with no talking. If you feel the need to say anything — and I advise against this unless you feel it absolutely necessary — then you simply repeat in a quiet but firm voice that it is time for sleep now. Nothing else.

If you are committed, if you follow the process I've explained above, and if you are utilizing the full power of Sleep Voodoo, then sleep *will* come. If you waiver, if you doubt, if you entertain any thoughts other than *you will sleep*, then sleep will not come. It's that simple.

The first night might be a battle of wills, a test of faith, but sleep *will* come. On subsequent nights, as the pattern becomes more ingrained, sleep will come easier and faster. Before you know it (sometimes in as little as two or three nights), you will be going from battles which last for hours to tucked in, kissed, and exited from the room in one smooth motion. Like I said before, this is much slower than the SAS Sleep Programme we're going to talk about in the next chapter, but it works.

Fixing Sam

I explained all this to Mark and Sarah who, being smart people, got it straight away. 'So now we have to make sure that you guys have a good routine in place, and you get rid of all the stuff that's been getting in the way of sleep.'

'What about the spoon?' Sarah stage-whispered. 'Do we just take it off her?'

I could see Sarah wasn't keen on just taking it, and the fury that would ensue. Now, whilst you never hold back discipline simply because you're scared of the reaction, you also don't have to blunder into every parenting decision like a stormtrooper. Why fight if you don't have to?

'The spoon? That's the easy part. The thing with little kids is that they're weird, all of them. Once you understand that, you can see the solution to just about any problem. Let me show you.' I turned to Sam. 'Hey, Sam?'

She looked up. 'Yeah.'

'I was just wondering how your spoon was feeling.'

She looked puzzled.

'I'm a spoon doctor. Lots of kids bring their spoons in for me to give them a check-up. Would you like me to have a look at it for you?'

She thought for a moment, then nodded shyly. She stood up and brought the teaspoon over to me. I took it from her and carefully laid it on a paper tissue on a chair in front of us. I made an effort of looking at it for a moment, umming and ahhing as I imagined a spoon doctor might. 'It's just as I thought,' I said. 'This is a very tired spoon. This spoon is the most tired spoon I think I've ever seen.' I picked it up and showed it to her. 'You see this?' I said, pointing to the curved handle.

She looked at it intensely, nodding.

'See how it bends in the middle there?'

Again the nodding.

'This spoon is so tired it's bending. In fact, this is one of the worst cases of spoon bending I've seen today. Does this spoon have its own bed at home?'

She shook her head. 'No.'

'Well, there you go then,' I said, handing it back to her. 'That's the problem. Would you like to help this spoon, Sam?'

She nodded. 'Yes.'

'This spoon needs its own little spoon bed. Do you think you could make one for it today?'

'Yes,' she said, clearly excited at the prospect.

'Good. You will need to make a very special, very comfortable little bed for this spoon, and then tonight, just before your dad tucks you in and says goodnight, I want you to tuck it in bed and tell it to go to sleep. OK?' Nodding. 'And if it tries to get out of bed, you tell it that it needs to stay in bed and go to sleep because night-time is for sleeping, OK?' Nodding. 'Good girl. I'm sure with someone as kind as you looking after it, this spoon will have a very good night's sleep in its own spoon bed and will feel much better in no time.'

I turned back to Mark and Sarah. 'You get the picture?'

They did, and off they merrily went.

I called them a few days later to learn that things were significantly better. The first night had been surprisingly easy. Sam had had her dinner, and a bath, and then changed into her pyjamas so she could help her spoon change into its pyjamas. Then they had a story on the couch in the lounge and went up to bed. As arranged, she had tucked her spoon into bed and then Mark had tucked her into bed, told her it was time to sleep, and sat quietly on the end of her bed. Sam had tried to talk to her dad a little, started to get a little grizzly, but then lay quietly in bed. When it looked as if she was drifting off, Mark had quietly left. Sam had come out of her room about five minutes later, bleary-eyed, but Mark had said nothing, made no eye contact, and gently but firmly took her back to bed. He sat there again for five minutes and left. She was asleep less than five minutes after that. For the first time in living memory, Sam was in bed and asleep by 7.30.

By the third night, all that was needed was a kiss and a goodnight and that was the end of it. No getting up, no dramas.

'It feels like a miracle,' Sarah said. 'Who would have thought such a simple technique could work so well?'

Who indeed?

The Soft and Gentle (but slower) Sleep Programme

Remember the three Rs: routine, routine, routine.

Get rid of anything that is going in the opposite direction of sleep (juice, television, lights, dancing bears).

When they are in bed, *tell* them that it is now time to sleep.

Withdraw as far away as you can before the child reacts (end of the bed, middle of the floor, the doorway), and then simply sit there without reacting or responding.

If they get out of bed, pick them up, put them back into bed, and withdraw to where you were again.

Anything other than getting out of bed you completely ignore. Lack of reaction from you is the key.

Wait patiently, remembering that there is now only one possible outcome . . . sleep!

As the child begins to settle, edge quietly from the room. If they begin to react, come back a little, then wait quietly again.

Enjoy the wonderful moment when you realize they've just nodded off.

The SAS Sleep Programme:
double bubble, twins are trouble

NEW REFERRAL	
Family details	Terry (29) and Shelley (28), and their twins Caitlyn (4) and Annie (4)
Presenting problem	Shelley describes bedtime as a disaster. The girls share a room and are a nightmare. They won't stay in their beds, make a huge racket, run around the house, and most nights don't get to sleep until somewhere between 9 p.m. and 11 p.m.
Notes	Sounds like parents are at the end of their tether with this one.

I *seriously* love these ones.

I'd imagine it's a bit like when a patient comes into a doctor's office with a huge growth in the shape of a flamingo sticking out the side of their head, like some bizarre lawn decoration on their face. A growth so hideous and uncomfortable that it's made the sufferer's life such a misery they'd given up any hope of ever being normal again, and then the doctor just reaches over and plucks it right off.

'How's that, then?' the doctor would ask, tossing the flamingo-sized growth in the bin with practised ease.

Cases like Terry and Shelley's are just like that, because it's a fixable problem which will make the people who've come to see me very happy indeed. And by golly I do like happy people. (Not all the time of course, because the chronically happy can be a bit wearying, but certainly in measured doses.)

'So paint me a picture of how bad it gets,' I asked after all the introductions had been made.

'Never have twins,' said Terry, shaking his head with the air of a man who's been to the dark side of bedtimes.

'No way,' I agreed. 'It's hard enough when they come along one at a time, but when two of them jump you it's going to get rough.'

Turns out it *had* got rough. Bedtimes were a total mess. It started out OK, but as soon as they got into their room it all turned to rubber chickens. The girls yelled and screamed and ran up and down and in and out and round and round.

'You must be going spare,' I said to Shelley. There was no need for a question mark. I was fairly confident a simple statement of fact was all that was required.

She nodded. 'The big difficulty is that, because there are two of them, if one gets settled then the other one stirs them up. Night-times in our house are total chaos.'

'How long has this been going on for?' I asked.

'Since they could climb out of their cots.'

'That's funny,' I said, 'because I just had an image of the Dr Seuss story about the Cat in the Hat and his two little helpers, Thing 1 and Thing 2. Is it like that?'

'Yup,' they both said, although they clearly didn't find the image funny so much as accurate and more than a little depressing.

'Shall we fix it, then?' I asked.

'Is that even possible?' asked Terry.

'It's more than possible — in fact, it's so probable it's practically inevitable.'

That's the problem with Dr Seuss: once you start thinking it, in the blink of an eye you'll be saying it too, unless you're a cow, when a moo must make do.

Where things went pear-shaped

This one is clearly a case of the problem being situated on the wrong pairs of shoulders. At the moment Terry and Shelley were the ones getting all stressed about it, while little Caitlyn and Annie were tearing round having a whale of a time. They had no reason to stay in bed and keep quiet, because there was far more fun to be had charging about and causing a commotion. To add to the problem, there were two of them so settling them the slow and gentle way, as described in the previous chapter, was probably not going to work. This required something a little more rigorous.

The SAS Sleep Programme

I have to admit at the outset that this is not an official SAS sleep programme. In fact, so far as I am aware, whilst the Special Air Service may have expert knowledge in demolition, hand-to-hand combat, hostage rescue, close surveillance, and hostage rescue, they probably aren't the best people to get advice from when it comes to getting small children to sleep. The real reason I call this the SAS Sleep Programme is that, like the SAS, it's very clear and direct, and it takes no prisoners.

Here's how it works:

1 Do all your normal bedtime things of baths, stories and wind-down.

2 When it's time for sleep, simply announce this, say goodnight, and slip quietly out the door.

3 If they stay in bed, all good.

4 If they run out of their room, tell them that if they aren't back in bed by the time you count to three you'll put them back in their room and lock the door.

5 Count to three.

6 If they aren't back in their room, pick them up, pop them back in their room, and then close and lock the door. Don't put them back in bed, just back in their room.

7 Wait for them to get upset (anywhere from one second to a couple of minutes).

8 After giving them a moment or two of being upset so they can get a taste of what life is like if you don't listen to your parents, open the door and tell them that, if they aren't in bed by the time you count to three, you will close the door again.

9 Repeat the process as many times as necessary until they get the point.

The big thing here is that the reason they get out of bed is to be close to you, and to have more fun. If you close the door the act becomes self-defeating, because they actually end up further away from you if they get out of bed. If they stay in bed then the door is open, the hall light is on, and they can hear you bustling about.

If you have more than one child in the room, as in the case of Caitlyn and Annie, then anyone who doesn't listen gets put in another room, say the laundry or the toilet. These places are generally very dull and nowhere near as cosy as a warm bed, and so children will quickly do the maths. The choice is simple: lie in my nice, warm bed, or get up and run around and then stand in the uncosy laundry.

Fixing Caitlyn and Annie

'It's that simple?' asked Shelley, slightly disbelieving.

'It is. All you need to do is make sure every time they get out of bed they end up in the laundry, and before you know it they'll be staying in bed. Laundries aren't much fun.'

'I'll give it a try but they're pretty full-on,' she said.

She did, they were, but it still worked.

'I can't believe it,' Shelley said two weeks later when we spoke on the phone. 'It took about two nights, and then they just stopped getting out of bed. Now we put them in about 7.00 and they talk for a bit and by 7.30 they're asleep most nights.'

'Cool, huh?' I said.

'Very cool,' she replied.

And it is. You don't have to bellow or chase them around, you just make getting out of bed their problem, not yours, and they start to stay in bed.

It isn't quite as dramatic as plucking a giant flamingo-shaped growth off someone's face, but it's bloody close I reckon.

The SAS Sleep Programme

Remember the three Rs: routine, routine, routine.

Get rid of anything that is going in the opposite direction of sleep (juice, television, lights, monkeys playing tennis).

When they are in bed, *tell* them that it is now time to sleep.

Say goodnight and leave.

If they come out, give them the three-count to get back into bed.

If they don't, put them back in their room and close and lock the door.

Wait until they sound a bit unhappy.

Open the door and give them another three-count to get into bed.

Repeat a few times until they get the message.

If they stay in bed, leave the door open and make sure they can hear you bustling about so they get a payoff for being good.

If you have more than one child in the room, remove the noisy disruptive one to a less cosy room like the laundry.

Once they do the maths and work out that staying in bed is far easier than getting out of bed, make yourself a cup of tea and watch something nice on the telly.

9

The bed thief

NEW REFERRAL	
Family details	Simon (29) and Petra (28), and their son Jordan (8)
Presenting problem	Petra described Jordan as a horror at night-time. He refuses to go to bed and will go only when Simon and Petra go. Even then, it is a struggle. They have tried everything and nothing has worked.
Notes	Things have slid a bit.

It always intrigues me when I get a referral and parents are saying they can't get their little one to do something. I mean, how big can an eight-year-old be?

Jordan had 'the look' as soon as I saw him — not spoiled, but certainly indulged. There was just something about him.

'Sleep has always been a problem with Jordan,' said Petra.

'How so?' I asked.

'Ever since he was a baby, we've had problems getting him settled.'

'Can you describe for me what you did when he was a wee fella?'

'You mean a baby?' Petra asked.

'Yes.'

It turned out they'd broken all the sleep rules. They'd walked him for hours, driven him to sleep in cars, fed him with milk, and abandoned any semblance of a consistent night-time routine. Sleep was something that came to Jordan only after exhaustion had laid a rather fragile groundwork. The only time he ever went to sleep by himself was when Petra and Simon had fallen asleep themselves out of sheer exhaustion.

'I see,' I said. 'And when he got older and moved from his cot to a bed?'

Simon's mouth affected a look of exasperation. 'He never really did move to a cot. Mostly he moved into our bed.'

I looked at Jordan, not a huge boy, but certainly quite tall for his age. 'I hope it's a big bed,' I said.

Simon shrugged. 'I mostly go and sleep in his room when he comes into our bed.'

'How often do you do that?'

'Every night.'

I frowned, thinking I must have got the wrong end of the stick. 'You mean . . . ?'

'Every night,' said Simon

'For how long?'

He shrugged again. 'Until morning.'

I shook my head. 'No, I mean how long have you been sleeping in his bed?'

'Since he was about three.'

Now, despite the fact that I'd failed two maths papers at university (one with an E, which is about the worst grade you can get if you're still breathing) even I could do that maths. 'Five years?'

Simon shrugged again. 'It's easiest that way. I can't sleep in the bed with him there. He has bony elbows.'

Jordan smiled as he looked down. I couldn't decide if it was a mischievous, good-natured grin, or something with more of an edge to it. 'Is this true?' I asked Jordan.

He nodded, but said nothing.

'Wow,' I said. 'Only eight and you managed to steal your dad's bed.'

'I didn't steal it,' he said, sounding aggrieved.

'You didn't?'

He shook his head. 'No.'

'Where did you sleep last night?'

He said nothing, but smiled self-consciously.

'I thought so,' I said, then turned back to Simon. 'And what does Simon say about that?' I asked.

'I don't like it obviously. We'd both prefer he sleeps back in his own bed.'

'What do you think?' I asked Petra.

'We've tried everything. We've read books, we've seen people. Nothing has worked.'

I didn't believe them. A lot of people say they've tried everything but closer examination usually reveals a problem in either the application or the follow-through. Usually 'tried everything' means we tried it for a couple of weeks and then gave up. The truth is that if you really have 'tried everything' then you would have found something that worked. Kids simply aren't that complicated — not even the really complex ones.

'Who was the last person you saw?' I asked.

When they told me the name, I recognized the person straight away. It was someone I knew — a very good clinician with years of experience working with kids. 'And what did he tell you to do?'

Petra explained that they'd been told to set up a system of rewards and consequences, all of it very sensible and practical stuff. So how come it hadn't worked? It turned out they hadn't followed through. The first night things had got rough, so they'd caved and let Jordan sleep in their bed again. They hadn't gone back to see the therapist again.

'OK,' I said, 'so what exactly do you expect me to do?'

'We just want some help, some kind of technique to help us get him to sleep,' Petra said.

'But you've already been given that. The last person you saw is very good at this stuff. The things he told you would have worked. The problem is you didn't do the things he said. I can tell you some things now that will help, but history says you won't listen and then you'll be sitting in someone else's office in six months' time telling them how I didn't help you either.'

I wasn't meaning to seem rude, but it was a waste of their time and mine if we were going to come up with a solution that would then be put in a box on the shelf with all the other solutions they'd been given. You can tell people, but they don't always listen.

'This time we really want to get on top of this,' said Simon.

'You say that now,' I said, 'but what about tonight when young Jordan here spits the dummy because you're taking back the bed? What's to stop you from caving in again?'

Simon jumped in this time. 'We really need to fix this,' he said. 'Jordan is getting older and this is getting ridiculous.'

'I agree,' I said. 'This *is* ridiculous. This boy is eight and he needs to be sleeping in his own bed at a sensible time. If you don't stop him from stealing your bed, then the next thing will be your car, your life savings, and your sanity.'

Simon nodded, smiling grimly. 'I know.'

Petra looked a bit more hesitant. They were both soft, but my guess was that she was the weakest link in this chain. 'If you let him steal the bed,' I said to her, 'the next stop is mayhem. You have to draw a line in the sand here and now.'

'I know,' she said, sounding weak and ineffectual. 'He just won't listen.'

And therein lay their biggest problem: wowser parenting.

I turned to Jordan. 'Stand up, wee man,' I said in my firm but polite psychologist's voice, and, because he's a kid and most kids are used to doing what they're told, he did. 'Now you stand up,'

I said to Petra, standing up myself so she wouldn't feel like a performing seal. She did, although she looked a little uncertain. 'Good. Now,' I said, looking at her and pointing to Jordan, 'pick him up, Mum.'

She smiled and frowned, uncertain if I was serious. I was. 'You mean actually pick him up?'

'Yup.'

'Why?'

I shrugged. 'Humour me. Pick him up.'

Frowning, she went to Jordan and, putting her arms around him, she picked him up without too much trouble. He was tall, but skinny.

Jordan giggled and squirmed a bit.

Petra put him down again, and looked at me.

'You see?' I asked her.

She frowned for a moment, and then smiled. 'Well yes, but—'

I shushed her quiet. 'You can yes-but me if you want, but yes-buts will not help you. You've yes-butted many times on the road to my room. Perhaps the time for yes-butting has passed?'

She opened her mouth, as if she was about to say something, then she closed it again, and simply nodded.

'OK,' I said, indicating to the chairs again, 'shall we deal to this bed thievery?'

She nodded again. 'Yes, please.'

Where things went pear-shaped

Jordan was a bed thief, that much was certain, but his parents made it all but impossible for him not to be. They were leaving the front door open and hanging a big sign on the front lawn, effectively saying: 'Hey, burglars, come on in and take our stuff. We won't complain.'

Remember: all kids need fences.

If you don't build fences, kids will run forward until they hit one. This is a basic principle of being a kid — you must always run forward until you get to the fence. Some of them simply need to see it, others need to collide head-on, but they all need the fence.

Jordan's parents had been steadily shifting the fence back until things had got to the point where they had given up their bed. If you sleep in your kid's bed and they sleep in yours, something has gone seriously wrong. There's nothing wrong with the occasional night where bad dreams, storms, or similar things drive them in there, but when they start moving their gear in for the long haul, you have to tend to your fences.

Simon and Petra had given in, shifted the fences too far back, and now things were all doo-lally. They were being wowser parents and they needed to harden up.

Sleep and big kids

As kids get older, the sleep problems tend to be more about pure compliance than the weirder things of little kids. Little kids will want to get out of bed because they have lost their spoon, or the chair is scary, or teddy wants to play. Older kids get out of bed often out of sheer bloody-mindedness. They don't tend to give you weird reasons; they just do it.

As with the previous examples, it is all about routine, technique, and also fences. Sleep with bigger kids is more blatantly about who is in charge. As a result, the plans you develop for bigger kids need to more bluntly utilize basic behaviour management principles, including the Golden Rule of Chapter 2 (Make it their problem not your problem). I'm going to talk about general behaviour management in a lot more detail later on, but just for now let's look at it in the context of Jordan and going to bed.

Simply put, Jordan was being rewarded for being a tyrant. If he dug his heels in and refused to go to bed, he was rewarded in three ways: first, he was able to reap the rich psychological pleasure that all children feel when they've got one over on their parents; secondly, he got to stay up later; and thirdly, he got heaps of attention.

What was needed here were some fences, and some consequences that had meaning for Jordan.

Fixing Jordan

'What do you enjoy the most in the whole world, Jordan?' I asked.

Because he had no idea that he was setting himself up, he simply told me. 'Soccer.'

'You like that the most?'

He nodded. 'Soccer is really cool.'

I could see it in his eyes — this boy was mad passionate about the game.

'OK,' I said, turning to his parents. 'When would you like him sleeping in his own bed?' I asked it using a tone which said that this would be no problem at all — they just had to choose the night. I used this tone for two reasons: first, to instil some confidence in both them and their son, and, second, because it was true.

They looked at each other, before Petra said, somewhat hesitantly: 'As soon as possible.'

'Tonight?'

She smiled as if she wasn't sure I was serious. 'If that's possible.'

I turned back to Jordan. 'How much do you like soccer again?'

This time he answered a little less certainly, because, being a very bright young man, Jordan had tumbled my game before his parents had. 'Umm . . . quite a bit.'

I laughed. 'You're a smart kid, Jordan. What do you think I'm going to tell your mum and dad to do?'

He gave me a conflicted frown, because he was pleased with

himself for figuring it out, but in the same breath absolutely opposed to the idea. 'That I can't go to soccer unless I stay in bed?'

I smiled broadly. I liked this boy a lot. 'Bingo.'

Simon and Petra exchanged a glance at each other. I'd seen it many times before. This was the we-couldn't-do-that-it-would-be-too-mean look.

'Don't you be doing that,' I warned them.

'What?' asked Simon.

'Giving each other the we-couldn't-do-that-it-would-be-too-mean look.'

'It does seem kind of tough,' said Simon.

This time it was my turn to shrug. 'Having your bed stolen by an eight-year-old seems kind of the opposite, don't you think? Makes you wonder if you might need to harden up a bit if you want to retake the high ground.'

'But he loves soccer,' said Petra. 'I'm not sure we could just take that away from him.'

Jordan looked at his parents, his expression becoming a little more relaxed, confident almost.

'He doesn't have quite the same hesitation in taking away your right to a good night's sleep,' I said.

As parents, we are all too soft at times. I'm as guilty of this as the next dad. Love undoes us — that and fatigue.

'So you're saying we should not let him go to soccer if he doesn't stay in bed?' asked Petra.

I nodded. 'Yup.'

She frowned. 'But what if he never gets to go to soccer again because he can't stay in bed?'

I shrugged philosophically. 'Think of all the money you'll save on fees.'

Jordan looked mortified — quite some achievement when you're only eight. 'I'm not going to miss soccer!' he exclaimed.

'Then I guess you'd better stay in bed tonight,' I said.

Simon was looking thoughtful. Of the two of them, I think he was the most fed-up. 'You're right,' he said finally. 'We've been too soft.'

Petra looked at him, surprised. 'You think we should do this?'

He nodded. 'Yeah, I do. This is ridiculous. Jordan can sleep over at other people's houses and stay in bed, just not at home. If we don't sort this out now, when are we going to?'

Jordan's mortification slid from mild type I to end-stage type II. 'But you can't stop me from going to soccer,' he said, his eyes teary and panicky.

'Oh yes, they can,' I said. 'They're your mum and dad. They can stop the sun from rising if they decide to.'

Simon turned to Jordan. 'We don't want to stop you from going to soccer, but if you don't stay in bed then we *will* do it.'

'But—' Jordan started to say.

'No, Jordan,' Petra broke in, arriving a little late to the party, but better late than never, as the saying goes. 'Your father is right. We've been too soft and that has to change. You need to stay in your own bed at night.'

'But—'

'So how do we work this?' Simon said, cutting across poor old Jordan's deepening despair.

It was simple really.

Every night they went through a night-time routine pretty much as I've described in earlier chapters: dinner, bath, a bit of free time, then some reading time in bed. Jordan was to go to bed at 8.00 and that was it. If he came out of his room for anything other than fires or independently verified vampire attacks, he forfeited his weekend soccer game. For each night that he stayed in bed he got a special 20-minute soccer practice with dad in the basement.

I rang them a week later.

'And?' I asked Petra.

'Unbelievably he's managed it every single night.'

I smiled. 'Well done,' I said.

'The first night there was a bit of a performance, and he did stand at the door and plead a bit.'

'What did you do?' I asked her.

'We did what you said. We hardened up. We told him if he put a foot outside the door he was going to miss out on soccer, and we meant it.'

'What did he do?'

'He carried on for about 20 minutes, which we ignored, then he went to bed. He got out of bed a few more times and complained, but each time it got a little less. When we went up to check him at 9.30 he was asleep.'

'Brilliant,' I said. 'You did it. The way you responded was absolutely spot on, and that's why it worked. You guys feeling better now?'

I could hear her smiling down the phone. 'About a hundred times better. Night-times are quite pleasant now instead of being a major stress.'

Again, who would have guessed?

Secrets of sleeping in big kids

Remember the three Rs: routine, routine, routine.

Just as with little kids, get rid of anything that is going in the opposite direction of sleep (juice, television, lights, computer games)

When they are in bed, *tell* them that it's now time to sleep. *Don't* negotiate once the time to go to bed has arrived.

If they get out of bed, apply a consequence that has meaning . . . which generally means they lose something that is very precious to them.

If they persist in getting out of bed, take them gently but firmly back to their room and then leave again.

Do this as many times as you need to (be prepared to go up to at least 1,000 times) until they get the message that they need to stay in bed.

If they do come into your bed in the middle of the night, carry out the same process.

Reward each successful night with something special.

Eating

Eating problems drive parents nuts. Whether it is fussy eaters, freaky eaters, or periodic fasters, the whole food thing can drive parents absolutely crazy.

Again, though, eating problems are amongst the easiest things in the world to fix. Eating problems basically fix themselves.

Don't believe me? Back in 1972, a bunch of football players were in a plane that crashed in the Andes Mountains. They were up there for a very long time with just the snow and each other. After the few chocolate bars ran out, they ate snow for bit, but then they did the maths — they realized that people can't survive on snow, and so in the end they ate each other.

Smart thinking. Hungry people eat. They'll even eat each other if it comes down to it. That's about all you need to know to fix any eating problem.

10

The little boy who wouldn't eat his greens

NEW REFERRAL

Family details	Paddy (33) and Karen (33), and baby Steven (18 months)
Presenting problem	Steven is very fussy and won't eat any fruit or vegetables. Hard to even get him to eat anything consistently. The only thing he seems to like is milk, which he apparently drinks by the litre.
Notes	This kid has a milk monkey on his back.

Karen was a good mum — I could see that right from the get-go — and Paddy was a typical first-time dad, hovering in a supportive role. They trundled into my room with wee Steven already sucking on a bottle. You can spot first-time parents a mile away — they always have a rucksack full of stuff.

'So your little guy's a bit fussy, then?' I asked.

Karen rolled her eyes. 'Fussy with a capital F,' she said.

'Tell me about it,' I said.

Steven was a great baby in almost every respect. He had a nice, even temperament, had always slept well, and was doing all the normal things you'd expect for a bloke of that age. The only thing he wasn't doing well was eating. It seemed Steven was making up for the fact that he was good in all other respects by collecting his pound of flesh at the dinner table.

'I can't get him to eat any vegetables,' said Karen. 'I can't even get him to put anything that's vaguely green into his mouth.'

'What does he eat?'

Steven's diet was a little out of kilter, but not too much. He had a bottle of milk in the morning before breakfast, at morning and afternoon tea, and at lunch and dinner time. Steven apparently enjoyed nothing more than a leisurely bottle of *Château Lait*, served lukewarm. In fact, he refused to start any meal without a bottle.

'He's like a milk-junky,' Karen said.

Actually, he was, but we'd get to that in a minute.

Steven would snack on things, but nothing in any great volume or with any consistency. He didn't really eat any vegetables, and would only sometimes eat bananas, finely chopped, not sliced.

'I'm exhausted at the end of meal times,' said Karen. 'I'm usually surrounded by all the wasted stuff I've made him that he's had a small bite of and then refused to have any more.'

I noted Paddy's relative silence. He'd been quite chatty at the beginning, but once we'd got onto the food stuff he'd gone quiet. Clearly this was more Karen's issue than his.

'What do you think, Paddy?' I asked.

He shrugged. 'He's a fussy little beggar, but he seems pretty healthy.'

I looked at Steven. He was happily playing with some blocks and looked as if he didn't have a care in the world.

'So what would you like to get out of coming to see me today?' I asked.

'We'd like some strategies to get him to eat properly,' said

Karen. 'I'd really like to get him eating some vegetables and more fruit.'

'OK then,' I said. 'Shall I tell you how to do that?'

'Yes, please,' she said.

I took a deep breath and began my standard eating-in-little-kids rave: 'Back in 1972, a bunch of football players crashed a plane in the Andes . . .' I said, lapsing into a well-worn routine. As I recounted my story of survival and cannibalism in the mountains, I watched Karen's face go a little paler, and Paddy start to smile more.

'Apparently,' I said, quite nonchalantly, 'rotten brains taste like cheese.'

Karen winced.

Paddy laughed out loud.

I guess it's a guy thing.

Where things went pear-shaped

Karen and Paddy had fallen into one of the oldest traps there is — they'd let their anxiety about eating manipulate them into becoming short-order cooks. They were so worried that poor Steven might not be getting enough to eat that they'd reached the point of making a hundred different things to try to get one thing in.

Steven was just a little fella, but already he was starting to get the idea that food was one way he could control his parents. Give him another couple of months and he'd have them turning backflips. Children learn quickly, and one of the things they learn the quickest of all is how to make us spin on the spot.

It's all about advertising and fear

The problem is that there are so many people trying to sell us stuff, and all of them are happy to trade on our fear. They tell us we need to drink 70 litres of water a day, and eat high-fibre, low-fat, high-calcium, salt-free, low-carb fruitbats.

Oh yes, and you'd better stay away from low-fibre, high-fat, low-calcium, salt-heavy, high-carb fruitbats. Those things are the kiss of death.

And when it comes to our children it's even worse, because we know that children are GROWING and that their BRAINS are DEVELOPING. If we don't feed them the SCIENTIFICALLY PROVEN RIGHT BALANCE OF NUTRIENTS they'll grow up STUPID and UGLY. And if they are STUPID and UGLY, they WON'T ACHIEVE to the best of their ABILITY and will have LOW SELF-ESTEEM.

If you were to believe all the crap you read on the packaging, you'd go mental. Apparently, not only do we need to eat 'essential amino acids' but we also need to wash our hair with them.

Then there are the people who will feed their children only GE-FREE ORGANIC food. These are the people who no doubt believe that the world is full of toxins and that we should all have colonics on a regular basis to 'cleanse' our bodies. I'm sorry, but as far as I'm concerned there are just some places that hot, soapy water is not supposed to go.

Personally, I like organic food, but not because I'm a hippy. I don't think GE food will kill me, but I do think the natural stuff tastes better. Just because something is GE-free doesn't mean that it's automatically good for you. There are plenty of things that are completely organic and GE-free that are bad for you: hemlock, black widow spiders, tornados, and great white sharks, to name but a few.

Advertisers understand all this. They play on our fear and our gnawing doubts. They appeal to the most unstable and neurotic parts of the human mind.

'If you don't mind the RISK of your baby growing up UGLY and STUPID, then feed it any old rubbish,' they say. 'But if you want him or her to grow up BEAUTIFUL and SMART, then feed your baby our SCIENTIFICALLY PROVEN stuff.'

Yeah, right. You can go put your scientifically proven stuff right where it has been clinically proven that the sun don't shine.

All this has a lot to do with why parents become so concerned about eating — the constant low-grade fear that we're not doing it right, that we are somehow letting our kids down. It is this anxiety that often proves to be the undoing of parents when it comes to establishing healthy eating habits in their children.

Before we get too much into that, though, let's pause to chat briefly about the Breast Nazis, because often that's where maternal anxiety about feeding is given a walloping kick-start.

Breast Nazis

I couldn't write a book like this without saying at least a little about the Breast Nazis. My wife and I went to antenatal classes for our first child. We were just as anxious and uncertain as the next couple, and so it seemed the sensible thing to do. Some of it was interesting. Most of it I suffered through, pretty bored, because everything was repeated eight times, and I *hate* having stuff needlessly repeated to me. Say it once; that's all I need.

There were only two parts of the course that aroused any real level of interest for me. The first was the area of pain management during childbirth — where there was some pretty clear politics advocating that epidurals are for wimps, and 'natural' childbirth was the way for any kind of decent mother — and the second was in the area of breastfeeding. They discussed breastfeeding in great detail, but said nothing about bottle-feeding. I asked why that was, and was told they were 'not allowed' to talk about bottle-feeding because they were supposed to encourage mothers to breastfeed. There were some pamphlets on a table in the corner about bottle-feeding — they just weren't allowed to talk about what was in them. It was something about a UN convention, or the WHO, or some other lot.

Isn't it funny? UN conventions can't stop genocide in the

Balkans, but they can stop people talking about bottle-feeding their kids. Maybe it was the WHO after all. Or maybe, as I suspect, it was the BNs — the Breast Nazis.

Now, don't get me wrong, clearly breastfeeding is by far and away the best thing for tiny people. The chemical composition of breast milk changes over time to better adjust to the needs of the baby. There are a lot more goodies in breast milk than you can ever get in formula. Let me be very clear in saying that, if you have the choice, breastfeeding is the way to go without any doubt at all. But to not even *talk* about bottle-feeding?

I detect the faint odour of Breast Nazis in there somewhere. The whole area of pregnancy and childbirth is rampant with politics, and none more so than the area of breastfeeding. Advocacy is fine to a point, but to not even explain the mechanics of bottle-feeding to people just about to have a child? Something about that stinks.

Too many mothers feel like failures because they can't breastfeed, and then they have to scrabble around trying to find out what they can do. Some women even worry that feeding their kids formula may actually harm them in some way. Often it is this anxiety that rolls on all the way through the feeding process, causing all kinds of problems.

Let me just say this: no baby ever died from being bottle-fed formula (unless it's been tampered with).

Salman Rushdie got in all kinds of trouble for writing unflattering things about the Prophet Mohammad. The Ayatollah took out a *fatwa* on him for that one. No doubt the Breast Nazis will be similarly offended and take out the lactation equivalent of a *fatwa* on me for saying this. (Would that be a *lacwa*, I wonder?)

Tough. I get tired of people trying to make parents feel guilty, whether it be intentional or not. A little while ago, I received an email from a very irate midwife who said that it was incredibly insensitive to say that no baby had ever died from being fed formula after all the deaths in China, when babies were given formula that had been laced with melamine. This particular midwife was so aggrieved, outraged, and appalled that she said she hoped I'd develop kidney stones so I could understand the suffering endured by those babies. Hmmmm. I'll say it again, and I'll say it with no reservations: no baby has ever died from being bottle-fed formula. I have never, on the other hand, advocated giving babies melamine. It's a poison. There is quite a difference between infant milk formula and poison, which I would have thought was kind of obvious.

If for whatever reason breastfeeding is not possible, we have to think about what is best for the well-being of both the baby and the mother. Feeling guilty for failing to breastfeed isn't good for anyone. It is, after all, the actual *feeding* which is the really important bit.

Which brings us nicely to the point that everyone needs to relax a bit around the whole food thing, and who are more relaxed about eating than dads?

Use dad psychology

Whilst we dads may have our faults (for example, the fact that we can't dress children in outfits that 'go together', or that we can't tell the difference between their good clothes and their everyday clothes, or that we can't brush their hair properly), we do tend to do some things pretty well. Dads tend to be a bit more relaxed about certain aspects of the parenting stuff — at least when their offspring are little. We can afford to be more relaxed, of course, because if it all goes wrong most people blame the mother anyway. Dads also tend to be out at work during the day, and so inherit the good behaviour when they get home after mum has put up with the crap all day.

One of the major areas of 'advanced paternal mellowness' is food. We dads tend to be pretty cool with the whole eating thing. If dad is in charge of morning tea, it probably isn't going to be anything that involves preparation. There will be none of the warm, freshly made food mum dishes up. Instead, there will likely be a handful of stuff in wrappers from the cupboard. There will be muesli bars, raisins, and foil-wrapped snacks. If the kids are lucky, there might be a plate. Most times there is just a cursory warning about dropping crumbs.

And the miracle of all this is that most children still somehow manage to survive dad morning teas without developing scurvy or losing an eye.

The other thing we do well with food is that we don't tend to worry so much if kids don't eat a lot.

'Look,' says mum, anxiety plainly evident in her voice, 'he hasn't eaten *anything*.'

Dad looks at the plate, searching for something to say to demonstrate that he is actually listening and that he is a concerned and committed parent. Having searched and found nothing — because he truly doesn't see what the big deal is — he simply shrugs: 'He'll be fine, don't worry about it.'

Mum gives him 'the look', the same one she gives him when he dresses the children in clashing colours and styles. Dad, realizing that simply not worrying about it isn't an option, suggests trying a banana.

'Is that your answer to everything?' she snaps. 'Try a banana?'

He shrugs again, feeling the ground slip away in that mysterious way that it always seems to do when he gets himself into trouble despite all attempts to the contrary: 'An apple?'

This stuff drives mothers crazy. They worry about vitamins, and nutrients, and scurvy and all manner of ailments. Dads, by and large, don't. Dads work on the perfectly reasonable logic that most children in the developed world don't starve to death. They work on the logic that, because they don't often hear on the news about the large numbers of children starving to death in their suburb and surrounds, this means it doesn't happen.

Consciously or not, dads work on the logic that hungry children eat. Dads proceed on the basis that if you don't eat your dinner nothing bad will happen.

Of course, the reverse of this is that dads can often be idiots as well. Dads can give kids sugary foods right before dinner which fill up little tummies just long enough to be a nuisance, and they can do other stupid things like letting the kids have dessert if they haven't eaten their dinner. So don't get me wrong: don't be too much like a dad, because dads can be idiots as well. But so far as trying to be more relaxed about eating — that you should do.

The three golden rules of eating for children

If you want to fix almost any eating problem in any little kid, you just have to remember the three golden rules:

1 Hungry children eat.

2 It takes about 20 yucks to get one yum.

3 Teach children to listen to their stomach, not look at their plate.

Hungry children eat

Fussy well-fed children don't eat. This is one of life's great truths. Fortunately for us, it is also one of life's great truths that hungry children *will* eat. Once the body burns up all the energy in the tank, the stomach starts sending messages up to the brain. These start as polite suggestions, but soon progress to desperate urges, then to strident demands, then all-out clamouring.

There is only one thing that makes a fussy child eat, and that is hunger. This is fantastic, because you don't have to do a thing to bring hunger on. In fact, all you have to do is wait. Waiting fixes about 98% of eating problems in little kids.

It might be true that you can lead a horse to water but you can't make it drink. However, it is equally true that eventually all horses get thirsty. Shortly after having had a drink, they will probably eat as well.

Thirsty horses drink.

Hungry children eat.

That's all you need to know.

The '20 yucks to one yum' rule

If you want your little one to go 'Yum, broccoli', you have to be prepared to hang in through about 20 doses of 'yuck, broccoli' first. This is not just my wingbat theory; this is what the boffins tell us after they've studied eating behaviour in children. On average you need to present a new food 17 to 20 times before a little person will try it. Twenty yucks to one yum.

The principle with little children is, therefore, multiple non-coercive presentations. If you want your children to try something new, you have to be prepared to wait. Even though it seems a sin in these times when we are constantly shown images of the starving in Africa, you also need to be prepared for a bit of wastage as well. If this makes you feel especially guilty, then ring World Vision and sponsor a child. Either way, you have to be prepared for the fact that you are going to throw food out for a while.

You present the new food to the child on a number of occasions without forcing them to eat it. Oddly enough, the number often turns out to be about 20.

It is *very* important not to force the child, since the single best way to create resistance is to try to make them eat it. If you push, they will push back. When this happens, the 20-yucks rule goes out the window and the number becomes ridiculously big. You do not want to get into forcing children to eat anything. This is very bad for a number of reasons, which I will talk about a bit more in the next section, but there is also the fact that it simply doesn't work. If you want Tarquin to hate carrots, then force them in his mouth while he is shrieking in protest.

Teach children to listen to their stomach, not look at their plate

If you ask someone with a weight problem when they stop eating, odds on the answer will be *when the plate is empty*. If you ask someone who is quite slim when they stop eating, odds on they'll say *when they feel full*.

People with a weight problem rarely leave anything on the plate. People who have no weight problem often will.

The difference between having a weight problem or not often falls down to whether you pay attention to what you see, or to the signals your body is giving you. Some people see stuff and they just *have* to eat it; other people see stuff and don't eat it because they don't *feel* hungry.

Childhood obesity is a growing epidemic, pardon the pun. This generation of children is the first in which the children are expected to die sooner than their parents. There are a number of reasons for this: a more sedentary lifestyle, higher calories in our food, lazy parents who can't be arsed cooking decent food for their kids, and the ready availability of processed junk on almost every corner.

Why do we have increasing rates of cancer, diabetes and heart disease? Because we eat too much, and not only that but — worse still — we eat too much processed crap as well.

As a result, it is vitally important that you teach kids how to eat properly. By this I don't just mean using a knife and fork and no spitting — I also mean how to eat the right kinds of foods and the right amounts. There are a ton of books about on what types of food kids need, so I'm not going to go into that now.

Eating the right amount of food is also easy. We come out with pretty good systems for limiting our food intake so that we get what we need. Age and experience, however, can screw that up. If you watch little children at a party, you'll notice something interesting: the younger children tend to eat less of the sugary crap than the older ones. Younger kids eat the sugary stuff until their stomach says it's full, then they tend to stop. The older kids tend to eat more of the sugary stuff because they have learned to override the signals from their stomach and focus more on what is in front of them. It's also true that children eat more if they are watching television — again, because their focus is on externals and not on the internal signals.

The upshot of all this is that you should never force children to finish the plate. You tell kids: 'You don't have to finish everything, you just have to eat until your tummy says it's full.' It's also good to point out that, once they say they've finished, there will be no more until the next meal, so they'd better have enough in their tummies to get them through — but you don't make them eat it all.

If you force kids to eat everything, you are setting them up for weight problems later in life.

In our house, our boys have always decided for themselves when they're finished. This doesn't mean that halfway through dinner you get down and play. If you're finished, you wait until the rest of us are done before hiving off and creating more chaos. Meal times are family times, and it's an important part of the routine of the day, not a quick snack-stop and off. The only thing we make the lads finish before they're allowed to get down is milk. You have to drink your milk. There is no negotiation on that one. Tantrums don't work. Stalling doesn't work. Nothing works. Finish your milk and then you can get down and play.

At times this has been a little hard for the boys' mother. Our youngest son sometimes eats like an anorexic sparrow. Sometimes he nibbles a side of something and that's it, literally — one tiny mouthful. My approach, being a dad, has always been that this will merely make him hungrier next time. He hasn't developed scurvy. No one from Africa has rung up offering to sponsor him for a dollar a day.

Hungry children eat. When he is hungry, he does eat. He might go through phases where he hardly touches a thing, and other times he tucks in like a Viking just back from pillaging. What we do know is that he has learned that you eat when your stomach tells you it's hungry, and you stop when it says it has enough on board to get the job done.

Whatever he will end up being — and I have a few ideas about that, not all of which are reassuring for his poor mother — fat will never be one of them.

Fixing Steven

Let's go back to the little boy who wouldn't eat his greens. The first thing was that the milk-junkie stuff had to stop. Steven had a monkey on his back and it was white and came from a cow. The problem with a bottle of milk before a meal was that it filled him up too much. He was going to be a lot less likely to try things if he had a bellyful of milk.

'But he'll throw a major wobbly if he doesn't get his milk,' said Karen.

I nodded. 'He certainly will.'

She looked as if she was waiting for me to say something else about the milk issue. I just shrugged.

'Oh,' she said. 'OK then.'

'The road to salvation in this particular case is paved with tears,' I said. 'My advice is dig in.'

Karen and Paddy looked at each other.

'The next thing is, we need to get out of the multiple-choice offerings at meal times. From now on, we eat what is put in front of us or we don't eat at all. This seems a bit harsh, I know, but you have to trust in the fact that hungry children eat. When Steven is hungry, he *will* eat. You just have to wait it out.'

'But what if he doesn't eat for days?' Karen asked, jumping ahead to the worst-possible scenario as if it was the obvious place to begin.

'Well, first off, that's fairly unlikely, and secondly you can stack the dice a bit. You can lean pretty heavily on presenting him with the stuff you know he likes to begin with, and introduce new stuff as a side dish. And remember,' I said, 'how many times do you have to serve a new thing up before kids will try it?'

'About 20,' said Paddy.

'Twenty is right. You have to be prepared for that. Serve up the carrot sticks at least 20 times without hoping he'll even look at them. Don't force him, just put them on the plate and let curiosity take its course. OK?'

They both nodded dutifully.

'Good. Now the next thing is we want to play a more strategic game so far as food is concerned. I want you to introduce fruit and vegetables as toys.'

Karen looked at me, confused. 'You mean . . . ?'

'I mean I want you to squish bananas between your fingers with him. I want you to roll oranges along the floor. I want you to hide behind lettuce leafs and play peekaboo with the broccoli trees.'

They both smiled, getting the point straight away. 'So we teach him to think of fruit and vegetables as fun, rather than something to fight about,' said Paddy.

'You got it. I also want you to read stories to him about food; not all the time, but sprinkled in with all the usual stuff you do.'

'So that's it then,' Karen said. 'Offer less choice, take away the milk before meals, and make food more fun.'

I nodded. 'Yup.'

'I guess it's pretty simple really,' she said.

'Yup.'

As they were leaving, I handed Karen a sealed envelope. 'Use this in emergencies,' I instructed her.

'What is it?' she asked.

'Instructions that you should follow the first time you find yourself worrying because he didn't eat any dinner. Call me if you get stuck.'

A month later, having heard nothing, I gave Karen a ring to see how things were going.

'Oh,' she said when I said hello. 'It's *you*.'

This didn't seem like the best of beginnings.

'How's it going?' I asked.

'It was a bloody nightmare,' she said. 'That first night he screamed for 20 minutes for his milk and then refused to eat a thing.'

I made a face at the other end of the phone, a grimace of sorts. 'Really?'

'Oh, yeah,' she said. 'He howled like a banshee.'

'What did you do?'

'Stupid me: I did what you said.'

'You ignored it and stuck to your guns?'

'Yeah.'

'Good for you,' I said, trying to be upbeat. 'And . . . ?'

'And that became the pattern after that. You'd think we'd taken away his left arm the way he complained. I thought he was going to pop each time we sat down to eat.'

'And the fruit and vegetables?'

She laughed. 'He mostly threw them onto the ground.'

'I see.' Again, the grimace. I was sure from her tone that she'd given up on my plan and gone back to the old ways. Now I'd be the one who she'd tell someone else hadn't been able to help them. 'So you want to make another time and we'll try to fine-tune things a bit?'

'No.'

Hmmm.

'O-K. So where to from here then?'

She laughed, and I could hear her tone soften. 'Today we tried carrots.'

I smiled, tentatively. 'That's great.'

'Not only that, but we've also discovered quite a fondness for bananas and grapes as well.'

'You're kidding?'

'No. We stuck to our guns just like you said, and it was horrible for a while, but then little by little he started eating things.'

'Fantastic. What do you think made the difference?'

'I think it was two things. First, we stuck to our guns and stopped giving him 18 choices, and secondly playing games with food really helped as well. Although having said that, we do still have a tendency to squish our bananas more than we actually eat them.'

I laughed. 'Call me if he's still doing that at 30.'

Karen assured me that she would.

(And, just in case you are wondering, inside the envelope I gave to Karen was a single piece of paper with one sentence written on it: *Hungry children eat.*)

Secrets of eating for little kids

Remember the three golden rules:

1 Hungry children eat.

2 Twenty yucks to one yum.

3 Teach kids to listen to their stomach, not look at their plate.

Don't offer multiple-choice meals.

Don't give milk or sugary snacks just before meals.

Stick to your guns and wait it out.

Play with food, make it fun.

11

The children made of chips and mushy peas ice cream

NEW REFERRAL	
Family details	Diana (33) and Kevin (33), Josie (9) and Tyler (7)
Presenting problem	Josie and Tyler refuse to eat anything but chips and something called 'mushy peas ice cream'. Refuse to even try anything else. Parents being driven spare by this.
Notes	Ask about the ice cream.

When you hear about kids who will only eat 'mushy peas ice cream', you just have to see them. The curiosity, in cases like this, would eat you alive if you didn't satisfy it. If I hadn't seen these guys, I would have gone to my grave wondering what mushy peas ice cream is.

'So what is mushy peas ice cream?' was obviously always going to be my first question. It turned out to be not such a good one.

Both kids frowned and looked at Diana, their mother, whose face went a bit red and who suddenly looked very uncomfortable.

Kevin, the dad, couldn't come to the session because he couldn't get time off work.

And, of course, in that instant I understood what mushy peas ice cream was. It was the way mum surreptitiously tricked her kids into eating vegetables — mushy peas mixed in with the ice cream. In that moment I realized I'd probably just blown her only way to get anything green into these guys.

I felt as if I was sitting in an East German café in 1976 and had just said to the guy next to me in a very loud voice: 'So, how long have you worked for the CIA?'

Bugger.

Now I'd have to get these kids eating greens because I'd just blown the existing deal out of the water.

'Mushy peas ice cream?' asked Josie, looking at her mum. 'What's that?'

'It's a joke,' I said, scrambling to recover the situation. 'What's mushy peas ice cream?'

Josie looked at me suspiciously. 'I don't know: what is mushy peas ice cream?'

I searched desperately for a punch line. 'Green,' I said, grabbing at the first word that came into my head, and affecting the world's most insincere smile.

The silence was so deathly I swear a tumbleweed blew through the room.

'That's not funny,' Josie observed rather dryly. Some kids are nine going on 14. Josie was one of those. Smart, articulate, and already working on adolescent disdain.

I shrugged. 'I know, I'm working on some new material. So anyway, what is it with you guys and food?'

'We don't like it,' she said.

'What . . . *any* of it?'

'We like chips,' Tyler chipped in helpfully.

'And?' I asked.

'And ice cream,' said Josie, shooting her mother a suspicious glance.

Diana, for her part, shot me a glance of her own.

With all this stuff flying about, someone was going to lose an eye.

'These guys just eat chips and ice cream?'

She nodded. 'That's right.'

'And that's it?'

'Unfortunately, yes.'

I looked at Josie. 'No lettuce? Broccoli? Carrots? No beans? No zucchini . . . the world's silliest-sounding vegetable? Surely you must eat zucchini?'

Tyler laughed, but Josie just ignored me. 'Mum?' she asked, and I could hear the tone in her voice like the low hum of an approaching truck.

'What, Josie?'

'Why do we always have *green* ice cream?'

I fought the urge to wince.

'It's lime-flavoured,' Diana replied, although everyone except poor old Tyler could smell the rat in that one.

At this point I could see that the whole mushy pea thing was never going to fly again. The door on that one had closed for good. It was probably just as well. Sneaking peas into the ice cream is not going to work in the long run, no matter how much you might want it to. Josie was never going to eat green ice cream again, and she'd also make sure Tyler didn't touch it. There was no more ground to be lost — I'd yielded it all with my first sortie.

Now, in moments such as these, when you've put your foot squarely in your mouth, I always feel it's best to shove the rest of the leg in, just to show the world you're not afraid. I'd already screwed things up about as far as I could, why not push it right out past the edge?

'Maybe it's green because of all the peas your mum puts in there?' I suggested.

Josie looked at her mother; even Tyler was looking confused. 'Is that true?' she asked.

Diana looked at me. I gave her my *I'm-really-sorry-I-didn't-mean-to-blow-your-cover-but-maybe-we-should-just-come-clean* look. She must have understood at least some of it, because she did just that. 'Well, I had to get you to eat vegetables somehow.'

'Ooohhhh yuck,' whined Josie. 'I'm never eating ice cream ever again.'

'At least that's something,' I said to Diana, who looked less than convinced.

Tyler sat there frowning. 'You bought pea ice cream?'

'*N-o-o-o*, dummy,' Josie snapped, 'she put the peas in herself.'

Tyler's frown deepened. '*Gross.*'

'How come you guys don't eat vegetables?' I asked, thinking the best thing at this point was to push on.

'They taste gross,' said Josie.

'Which ones?'

'All of them.'

'*All* of them? You've tried every vegetable there is and don't like *any* of them?'

She wrinkled her nose. 'I don't try them.'

'So how do you know they taste gross if you haven't tried them?'

'You can tell from looking at them. Snot is green — would you eat that?'

'Some people do,' I said. 'Frogs are green as well, and the French have been eating them for years.'

Tyler laughed. 'Maybe we could have snot ice cream?' he said.

I liked Tyler. 'You think it would be smooth or would it have little sticky lumps in it?' I asked. He laughed again.

'Could you guys scoot out for a bit so I can chat with your mum?' I asked, wanting to end that bit in a little more upbeat, albeit slightly gross way.

Out they duly scooted.

'Sorry about that,' I said to Diana. 'I guess the ice cream thing is kind of blown now.'

'So what do I do?' she said, sounding slightly desperate. 'That was the only way I had to get any vegetables in them. They won't even try anything that looks like a vegetable.'

'Do they eat fruit?'

'Only apples sometimes, and even then the skins have to be peeled and all the pips removed.'

'Hmmmm,' I said. 'I can see why that would be a worry for you. Tell me how all this got started.'

It turned out that the Breast Nazis had a modicum of responsibility for this one. Diana had had trouble breastfeeding Josie at the beginning, and Josie had real problems putting on weight. 'I used to dread feeding her,' Diana said. 'I'd want her to have some milk, but I used to feel so useless and stupid because I couldn't produce enough for her.'

That set a bit of a pattern, in that feeding became a constant worry for Diana. The end result of this was that she'd just want to get anything she could into the kids.

She went through the whole multiple-choice meals thing with both Josie and Tyler. By the time Josie started school, the wheels had completely come off the cart.

Meals were a three-ring circus where the little people dictated what constituted an appropriate meal. It wasn't long before mum was up three nights a week surreptitiously grinding the peas into the ice cream.

If you let them, your children will have you acting like a mad person in no time at all. Grinding peas into ice cream in the dead of night is something only a mad person would do.

'So,' I said, after the history had been duly sorted through, 'shall we fix this problem then?'

Diana nodded. 'Yes, please.'

I took a deep breath: 'Back in 1972, a bunch of football players crashed a plane in the Andes . . .'

Where things went pear-shaped

You already know what I'm going to say, right? We know that the thing which set it all off was anxiety over feeding, and that led Diana to compromise herself all the way out of the rational world. She gave ground all over the place just to get them to eat, and sure enough they did what children do: they evolved their own completely mad rules. Chips and ice cream.

Again, you can't blame them: it's their job to be nutty. It's *our* job to teach them to curb the nuttiness and at least pretend to be sane like the rest of us.

Josie and Tyler said they didn't like vegetables, but that wasn't true. They didn't actually know, because they'd never really tried them.

I went through most of my adolescence absolutely convinced that I hated rhubarb. I politely declined it for years in complete certainty that it was not for me. Then I actually tried it. I can't remember why now, or even where, but I know that I must have tried it because at age 16 or thereabouts I discovered that actually I *loved* rhubarb. I kicked myself for all the rhubarb-less years, and from then on I gorged myself on the stuff whenever I could.

Josie and Tyler didn't hate green stuff — they'd simply tacked a whole bunch of negative thinking onto the idea of green stuff.

All we had to do was change that.

Eating does not have to be a stress

There are many things about raising kids that are almost inevitably a stress. Bad behaviour can be a stress. Lack of sleep can be a stress. Starting school can be a stress.

Eating does not have to be a stress.

Like I said before, eating is a problem that fixes itself. All you have to do is wait, weather a few tears and protests, and simply hang in there. They'll complain, but they'll also eat.

The simplest way to not get stressed is simply *not to*.

You must hold the knowledge in your head that hungry people eat. If you don't believe me, go get the book *Alive* by Piers Paul Read about the football players stranded in the Andes. If ever there was a clearer demonstration of the fact that hungry people eat, it is that story.

If you don't want to get stressed about eating, then don't.

Another way to think about it is this: if you were of a mind to starve your children, and you instructed them that they were not to eat the chicken salad that you put in front of them each night (and please understand that I am not advocating starving your kids as an intervention), how skinny do you think they'd get before they disobeyed you and started tucking in? How long would they sit there starving before they decided that disobeying you and eating the chicken salad was better than death?

If you wanted to stop them from eating, how long do you think you could do that for?

I'd bet it wouldn't be all that long.

Fixing Josie and Tyler

'OK, Diana, shall we sort these guys out then?' I asked.

She nodded. 'If you think it's possible.'

I laughed, 'Everything's possible.'

'So what do I do?'

'Simple: throw out all the chips in the house, and refuse to buy any for at least a year.'

Diana's mouth fair dropped. 'You're kidding!'

I shook my head. 'Nope. See,' I said, pointing, 'this is my serious face.' I paused and put on my serious face. 'This one, on the other hand,' I said, pointing again, 'is my kidding face.' I crossed my eyes. 'When I said chuck out the chips, I had my serious face on: this one here.' I put it back on again and pointed to underscore the point. 'See?'

'But what will they eat?'

I shrugged. 'There are two possibilities from here. The first is that they'll eat nothing. The upside of that is that if you're lucky Bob Geldof will think there's a famine on and throw a concert for you and invite Bono and Pink Floyd around for a concert in your back yard. The second possibility — and I have to say I think this one is a little more likely — is that they'll eat what you give them.'

'But I've tried that before,' she said, sidestepping the wit and heading straight for Anxietyville, 'and it's never worked.'

'I know,' I said. 'You told me. Except what you've done is put the vegetables on as a side dish and then caved in when they refused to eat the good stuff.'

'But they won't eat anything, I know they won't.'

'If you threw out all the chips and served nothing but healthy food for a year, I can guarantee you that they wouldn't go more than about 24 hours without eating.'

'Just do it cold turkey?'

'Cold turkey, warm turkey, do the turkey any old way you want. Just no chips.'

Diana sat back in her chair and worried. 'That seems pretty harsh,' she said.

'I know,' I said, softening a little, 'but if you want to get these guys to eat better, then you are going to need to take away the easy option. If you offer them chips, they will always take chips. At the moment they are on a diet that is going to put them at much higher risk of colon cancer, obesity, and heart disease. If they wanted to smoke, would you let them?'

'No, of course not.'

'This is the same thing,' I said. 'Poor diet is a killer.'

I wasn't trying to scare her: it was true.

She nodded. 'You're right, of course you are.' She sighed. 'I'll do it; the chips are gone.'

'Good, now let's get a bit of a plan together.'

Between us we worked out a menu. Instead of their usual sugary crap cereal we substituted a healthier cereal, wholemeal toast, and orange juice. Lunch was going to be variations on sandwiches, wraps, and different fruit. Dinners would be the biggest challenge.

'The trick is in changing their perceptions about food,' I said. 'You want to make them see green stuff in a different light.'

'But how do I do that?' Diana asked.

'That's where we test your creativity,' I said. 'One of the easiest ways is to involve them in the preparation of the dinner. Make cooking fun. Teach them how to make a salad and some kind of simple dressing. Teach them how to marinate chicken. Choose recipes that are exotic and fun. Skewer things on stakes and barbecue 'em. Build a campfire in the backyard and cook like cowboys.'

Diana nodded — she had that distant look of a mother hatching a cunning plan. 'I get it,' she said. 'So, like do things with food that draws them in rather than makes them screw up their noses?'

'Absolutely. Although the truth is that even if you just stopped the junk and served up healthy stuff, they'd cave and eat it anyway. It's just this way you start to change their whole relationship to food, plus you can educate them along the way about the kinds of foods they should eat to be healthy.'

I could see that Diana was quite excited about this idea. After years of food being a grind, she seemed to relish the idea of making it fun and interesting again.

'OK,' she said, 'I'll do it.'

And to her immense credit she did. Diana went home that night and, amidst the howling protests of her two little dears, she binned every last chip in the house. She also binned the sugary crap cereal, and the fatty, empty-caloried snacks that the kids had loved so much.

For their part, they were aghast. I'm sure Josie thought her mother had gone mad.

That night they both refused to eat dinner (a hastily assembled pasta dish) and went to bed hungry. Diana worried about that, but stuck to her guns. Next morning it was healthy cereal, wholemeal toast, orange juice, and political protests. Josie wasn't happy. Tyler did eat some toast. That night things weren't a lot better — more protests and very little eating.

By the end of the first week, there was some progress. Both kids were eating, but not very much. In a fit of anxiety Diana took them both to the doctor on day five. The doctor said, although obviously in a far more medically correct way: 'They're fine.'

By the end of the first month, both children were eating better amounts. In the absence of chips and mushy pea ice cream, they had no choice but to get with the programme.

Diana ended up doing several very creative things with the kids to get them involved with food. She made it part of the night-time routine that everyone helped with the dinner in some small way. Amazingly, Josie actually discovered quite a passion for cooking as time went on. Diana also bought some new cookbooks and said the children could choose which meals they wanted, taking turn about. The only catch was that they had to help make the meal as well. She also made a weekly competition that she called 'the world's weirdest vegetable' where the person who chose and ate the weirdest vegetable they could find at the supermarket won a double movie pass. Whilst slow to begin, the competition became fierce once it got going, to say the least. In the end, Diana was forced to take the kids to an Asian grocery store as the demand for more exotic vegetables soon outgrew their local supermarket.

After six months, home was a different place. Vegetables and fruit had become part of the family landscape. What's more, the taste for exotic dishes seemed to be developing at an exponential rate.

'Tonight Josie is making sushi,' Diana said, the last time I spoke to her.

'Ye gods.'

'I know,' she said. 'I would never have believed it possible, but there you go.'

'There you go indeed.'

'The other nice thing is that I've noticed a real change in their behaviour as well.'

'How do you mean?'

'They're both a lot more settled, not as flighty and emotional. Even their schoolwork is better. Both of their teachers have said that the kids are more settled in class and are doing better generally.'

I smiled. 'Fantastic.'

Who would have guessed, when kids eat healthier food, and less of the empty-caloried highly-processed crap, they feel, act, and learn better?

'The funniest thing is that next week is Tyler's birthday, and you know what he wants?'

'What?'

'Mushy peas ice cream.'

Secrets of eating for big kids

Let me say it again . . . remember the three golden rules:

1 Hungry children eat.

2 Twenty yucks to one yum.

3 Teach kids to listen to their stomach, not look at their plate.

Don't offer a choice between the good stuff and the crap – ban the crap outright. The only choice is the good stuff: it's either that or starve.

Involve your kids in food – find creative ways to make food interesting and fun.

Above all involve your kids in preparing the food they eat. They don't have to cook a three-course meal, but they can make a salad or marinate some chicken. You'll get better buy-in if they've helped prepare it.

12

Mother's mirror, Daddy's dustbin

NEW REFERRAL

Family details	Sandra (43)and Max (45), Evan (11), Emily (10), and Stephen (8)
Presenting problem	Parents having real troubles with Emily and eating. Mum thinks Emily may have an eating disorder, obsessed with diets and being skinny. Boys eat fine, no problems with them apart from normal boy stuff.
Notes	Fat cats with skinny kids?

They were an immaculate family. Being a scruffy soul by nature, I felt a bit underdressed. Mum was all designer this and shiny that. Emily was resplendent in pink and trendy washed denim. Dad had the look of a wealthy guy trying to be casual but really wanting to look like a rich guy. In contrast to the women in the family, who looked kind of skinny, dad had a fat-cat waistline.

'So, what brings you all along?' I asked, at the same time thinking *I bet a late-model Mercedes brought you guys along.*

'We're worried about Emily,' Sandra said.

Emily rolled her eyes.

'What specifically are you worried about?'

'She's obsessed with dieting,' said Sandra, 'absolutely obsessed.'

'No, I'm not,' Emily muttered.

'Oh, come on, Emily, tell the truth,' Sandra said. 'You *are* obsessed with dieting.'

'I'm *not*.'

Sandra rolled her eyes now. 'This is the problem. Every time I try and talk to her about it she does this.'

There was something about the way they talked to each other that really bothered me. They were all caught up in the 'I'm right — you're wrong' cycle, but there was something more than that. It was very subtle, but it was there, an underlying current of disconnection.

'What do you think about all this, Max?' I asked.

He shrugged. 'The diet issue is significant,' he said in very even tones. It sounded as if he was talking about a 10-point drop in the commodities market.

I looked at Emily. 'Do you know what that means?'

She shrugged.

'It means your dad thinks it's a big problem,' I said, then I looked back at him. 'Do you always talk like that?'

'Like what?'

'All complicated.'

He frowned a little, looking irritated. 'I didn't think it was complicated.'

I pointed at Emily. 'She's 10.'

He frowned. 'I know.'

I wasn't so sure he did, but I let it go for the moment. 'When did all this start?' I asked them.

Sandra spoke: 'She's always been picky, but the real problems started when she was five.'

'How so?'

'When she started school she became very difficult around clothes and what she would and wouldn't wear.'

I nodded, a proper shrink's nod, just the thing to nudge the story forward a bit more without the need for the painful 'ah-hah' or 'I see' or, the worst of all, 'Please continue.'

'Soon after that she started getting very fussy about her food as well, saying that she didn't want to get fat.'

I almost winced. 'At five?'

Sandra nodded. 'At five.'

Now there are a few things about that which raised my psychological heckles. At five, little kids do pretty much what they see around them. They are sponges. So where was all this 'eating makes you fat' and 'I don't like the way I look' stuff coming from? School or home?

'What do you like to eat?' I asked Emily.

She shrugged. 'Nothing.'

'Not even chocolate.'

She sneered, although more at the calories than at me. 'Chocolate makes you fat.'

I looked at her. 'You look as though you could eat a chocolate factory and you'd still be skinny.'

'That's what I tell her,' said Sandra. 'The women in our family do have a tendency to put on weight, but you just have to be careful. Emily could put on at least two or three kilos and still be fine.'

This time I did wince. That answered the question: home.

'So what have you tried to help her eat more normally?' I asked.

'I told her if she puts on a kilo I'll buy her some make-up,' said Sandra.

The wince became a grimace, which — realizing it had just over-extended itself — pulled itself back into a frown. 'OK, then. I wonder if we might have a wee chat while Emily reads a magazine out the front for a bit.'

After the girl had left, I focused on Sandra first. 'Do you like the way you look?' I asked her.

'Pardon me?'

'Do you like the way you look? Are you happy with your body shape?'

She laughed, embarrassed. 'I don't know. I suppose. Not really, not completely.'

'Are you on a diet at the moment?'

She positively shuffled her feet. 'Just a little one.'

'Are you on "little ones" very often?'

'I put on weight really quickly if I don't watch myself.'

I looked at her. 'Give yourself a score out of 10,' I said.

Dad was sitting there giving me this slightly amused smile. It didn't matter — he was next.

'You mean . . . ?' Sandra asked, confused.

'I mean: if you were to give yourself a score out of 10 for how good you feel about your own body, what would it be?'

She thought for a moment. 'Six. No . . . five. Maybe some parts a four.'

'OK. And you?' I turned to Max.

He laughed, a fat-cat laugh. 'You mean how would I rate my body?'

I nodded. 'Yup.'

Amazingly, his mobile phone went off at that precise moment. 'Excuse me,' he said, holding up a finger. I didn't excuse him, but he was already gone. After about a minute or so of schmoozing some business guy on the other end of the phone, he hung up. 'Now,' he said, 'where were we?'

'Out of 10?' I said.

Max flipped me a great big fat-cat smile: 'Ten.'

Who would have guessed?

'Right then, so you want her to eat more?' I said to Sandra.

She nodded. Max sat with a curiously mixed expression of amusement and disinterest.

'Listen carefully,' I said in my best professional voice, 'I want you to go and score about a kilo of cannabis — the good stuff, not just dregs — and then about a half-hour before each meal I want you to sit down with Emily and get her rat-faced stoned.'

Sandra looked as if I'd just sprouted a chicken from the top of my head. Max was frowning.

'That way,' I said, continuing merrily on, 'by the time the munchies set in it will be time for dinner and she'll eat anything you put in front of her.'

I smiled triumphantly. *Look how clever and wise I am*, the smile said. I swear, if a pin had been dropped, the sound would have echoed in the silence that ensued.

Where things went pear-shaped

The problem here was that Emily was doing what she was raised to do. She had been brought up to think poorly of herself, to scrutinize and look for imperfections, and to take drastic action. Emily was a product of her environment.

She had a mother who was a victim of the body-image industry, and a dad who wasn't doing his job. My impression was that Max gave the wife and kids the scraps left over after all the deals had been done.

A father's job is to provide for his family. That's what we are supposed to do. We provide for them, we keep them safe, we try the best we can to make them feel good about themselves, and we make them feel secure in the belief that, no matter how confusing the world might be, there will always be home. There will always be a seat to sit on, and an ear to listen.

I will always be here, no matter what happens to you, or what you do. You can always know that this will be true.

Providing a late-model Mercedes for your family is one thing, but a seat, some attention, and an ear is a whole other thing again.

On top of this heady mix, Emily had soaked up the popular culture stuff that leaked into her world from television, the internet, magazines, friends, but most of all from the conversations in her own home. Emily had been taught to worry about her weight, and then left to figure it all out by herself. Sandra's own preoccupations with kilograms and kilojoules had begun to poison her daughter as well as herself, whilst all the time Max was too busy closing deals to spend much time talking with his family and figuring out what was really going on.

It is *all* about relationship

There is absolutely no escaping the fact that raising children is all about relationship. The quality of the relationship you build with your children is the single most important thing you should be concerned about. You also need to be aware that children copy what they see. If you're an angry person, for instance, you are likely to have angry children. Copying the big people is how they figure out what to be in the world.

If you obsess about your weight, if you think you are too fat, then you are likely to pass this on to your kids. To be fair, not all this is down to parents — a lot of it comes from the popular culture stuff — but you can certainly make things worse. Your children watch what you eat, when you eat, and how you eat, and they start watching early.

Your relationship with yourself will influence your children's relationships with their selves.

Many girls, and increasingly more boys as well, struggle with body image. This is an issue that will not go away. You cannot hide from it, or pretend it isn't there. If you have kids, you have to teach them to feel good about their psychological selves *and* their physical selves.

Fortunately though, this doesn't have to be a big grind. Like anything, playfulness is the key.

Fixing Sandra, Max, and even Emily

'I'm not giving my child drugs,' Sandra finally said.

I feigned surprise: 'Why not?'

She laughed, a little uncertainly, much as one might if stuck in a small space with someone you're not sure is completely right in the head.

'Because that's silly.'

I shrugged. 'So? You want her to eat, don't you?'

'Yes, but . . .'

Max at last awoke from his disengaged slumber: 'Because it's illegal, and we're not going to give our daughter drugs.'

Thank goodness he'd finally showed up.

I shrugged again. 'It's a good idea, though.'

He frowned, looking annoyed. 'No, it isn't. If that's the best advice you have for us, then we've obviously wasted our time.'

I looked at him and smiled, softening just enough to get the job done. 'You know this is the first time you've come into the conversation since you got here,' I said, genuinely pleased.

Max frowned again. 'Well, that was a ridiculous thing to say.'

I waved a hand, 'Of course it was.'

'Then why did you say it?'

'Well, let me ask you this: aside from the fact that drugs are illegal, why else wouldn't you give Emily cannabis?'

'Because drugs are bad for her.'

I nodded. 'Exactly. And you wouldn't do something that was bad for her, right?' They both nodded.

'So why do you talk about food and weight the way you do in front of her?' I asked Sandra. 'And, Max, why do you take work calls when we're here trying to figure out a way to get your daughter to eat normally?'

'Are you saying this is all our fault?' Sandra said, sounding offended.

I didn't blink. 'Some of it is, yes — maybe even a lot of it. I'm not sure exactly where the line is drawn between how much is the world's fault and how much is down to you guys, but you're in there for sure.'

They looked a bit crestfallen.

I often wonder how the world ever got to the stage where nothing is ever anyone's fault. How did it get so out of whack that a 10-year-old girl could start down the road to an 'eating disorder' with her parents thinking it was somehow nothing to do with them?

'Don't take it so badly,' I said. 'You're her parents. It's your job to screw it up. We all screw it up in our own ways. I'm just as guilty of that as the next dad. The trick is that, when you see the ship is getting off-course, you correct it. The only time you should feel guilty is if you know it's going pear-shaped and you do nothing to fix it. You aren't those people, because you're both here trying to fix things. Right?'

They nodded.

'OK then, shall we fix this?'

'Yes,' said Sandra.

The fix in this case was two-pronged. The first issue to be dealt with was the food/weight stuff.

'When you get home tonight, I want you to go take the bathroom scales and throw them in the bin.'

This was clearly a rough session for poor Sandra. 'Actually throw them out?' she asked.

'Yup. You and Emily are far too focused on the little numbers. She doesn't need to focus on numbers and think about what the little numbers tell her about herself. She needs to focus on developing a healthier connection with her body. Little numbers just further disconnect her from this internal physical focus. Get rid of the scales.'

Sandra nodded. 'OK.'

'Then I want you to change the whole way you do food, from top to bottom.'

'How do you mean?'

'I mean all the fad diets are gone. Atkins died obese and the company went under. Give it all up. Ninety-something per cent of people are back at their original weight two years after a diet. Give it up.'

'So what do we do instead?' Sandra asked.

'Simple. What you do is eat healthy, exercise, and get some help to feel better about yourself. Then you help Emily to feel better about *herself*.'

'You make it sound so easy,' she said.

'I know it's not quite as straightforward as that, but there are lots of good places you can get information from. I can give you the name of a good nutritionist and also some books which can help as well. The secret with weight is getting your head in the right space, eating good stuff, and exercise. That's all it takes.'

Sandra, to be fair, looked less than convinced, but I'd make sure she went away with some definite steps to take.

'As for you,' I turned to Max, 'how much time do you spend talking to Emily every day?'

He shook his head. 'Probably not as much time as I should,' he said.

'I know what it's like,' I told him. 'It can be pretty hard to find time some days. You work your arse off all day, and when you get home all you want to do is collapse in a chair and watch crap on television. The problem is you have a daughter who needs you, so you can't. I want you to schedule in time every day to spend with her. It doesn't have to be hours, but she at least has to know that you're there. If you don't build a stronger connection with her now, then her adolescence is probably going to be a nightmare.'

Max nodded. 'I know, you're right.'

'Heck, yeah, I'm right. I have a bunch of degrees in this stuff.'

He laughed.

'Let me tell you both the secret of building relationships with grumpy kids: *ask questions*. Don't tell her what to think or how she feels: *ask* her. Teach her to talk about her feelings. Teach her that you will listen calmly to what she has to say. Teach her *how* to solve problems rather than telling her what to do. Every time you feel like telling her something, stop yourself, edit out 50% of it, and put a question mark on the end.'

They were both listening.

'And the last part of this,' I said, 'pointing to Max's fat-cat waistline, 'is that I want you to get on the healthy-eating/exercise train. This is going to be a family thing, OK?'

He laughed, and patted his stomach. 'I suppose I could get myself into slightly better shape.'

'Maybe less round?' I asked, smiling.

He laughed. 'Maybe.'

To their credit, they went away and jumped into it with both boots on. The scales went in the bin as instructed. Mum dumped her diets and bought some books on healthy eating. The family stopped having meals on the run, and sat down together. Everybody ate the same stuff. They started having 'family walks', and Emily became something of a personal trainer for her father.

They all worked hard to find their way back to a normal relationship with food, and with each other. The fixation on numbers on the scales was exchanged for spending time together. Some of that time was even spent cooking. Sandra took Emily to see a visiting celebrity chef one night and the girl was smitten.

'She actually has a picture of him up on her wall,' Sandra said.

I laughed. 'That wasn't exactly what I meant when I said develop a better relationship with food.'

Emily still wasn't the world's greatest eater, but she was starting to develop a healthier view of herself, her body, and food. Even better, she was actually talking to her mum and dad. They had started being a family again, rather than a bunch of related people fighting over their calorie intake.

Food, body image, and problems

First off, always remember that the *most important* job you have to do as a parent is to develop a strong relationship with your children.

Remember, too, that your children will pick up many of your beliefs and attitudes about all kinds of things, including food and body image.

If you don't want your kids to have a problem with eating, put your own shop in order first.

If you have girls, even if you have boys, home is no place for obsessive fad dieting. Don't model crazy weight-obsessed behaviour. The world will do that more than enough — it doesn't need any more input from you.

Teach your kids to eat healthy food — to listen to their stomachs not look at the plate — and to like themselves.

If you are really worried that your child may have serious issues with eating, get a phone book, look up the experts, and go talk to someone. Don't freak out, don't freak your child out, just quietly go off and have a chat with someone who knows about this stuff.

Number ones and number twos

Toilet-training. It isn't the most exciting thing in the world to think about. When most people dream out loud with their loved one about having children, it isn't the thing they automatically go to first: 'Won't it be *lovely* when we're toilet-training.'

Nope, it won't be. Actually it'll be stinky and pretty gross. But we all have to do it. This is just one of those jobs — so to speak — that has to be done. It can also drive parents potty though (heh heh!), so we need to have a quick look at this one.

Just a quick look, though. I'll give you everything you're likely to need for this one as quickly as I can, and then we're best to move on to sweeter-smelling pastures.

When number twos are involved, it has been my experience that you don't want to be hanging around too long.

13

Winnie the pooh-less

New referral	
Family details	Mandy (26), Kim (almost 4)
Presenting problem	Mandy has been struggling with toilet-training. Kim shows no interest, and it has become a huge battle in the house. Refuses to sit on the toilet and doesn't want to give up her nappies.
Notes	Ask about the grandma factor.

One of the many things about having children that amazed me was that new-baby poop smells a bit like cookie-dough. Maybe it was just our kids, I don't know, but for a while at least poop wasn't that bad.

Unfortunately, though, at a certain point all that changes. The slightly sweet-smelling cookie-dough mixture is replaced by stuff that looks and smells like it was scraped from the bottom of a rancid pond in Chernobyl. Children can look like angels on the outside, but there's obviously some pretty heinous stuff going on inside — something that almost always seems to involve both radioactive industrial waste and raisins.

All of which drives parents forward to the day when they will no longer have to be involved in this aspect of their kids' lives. There are a lot of things that it is fun to be involved in with kids, but poop is not one of them.

Mandy was utterly fed up with the whole thing. She obviously wanted Kim toilet-trained as soon as possible. Indeed, it was pretty clear from the start that she thought the lack of progress was a big problem.

'She just refuses to sit on the toilet at all,' she said. 'I end up trying to hold her there and she's screaming and howling. It's very stressful.'

'I'm sure it is,' I said. 'How did you decide that it was time to start toilet-training?'

'My mother was on my case about it a bit. She said that when we were kids we were toilet-trained by the time we were three. Kim's nearly four and she's still in nappies.'

Ah, I thought, grandparents and toilet-training.

'So your mum thinks Kim should be out of nappies?'

Mandy nodded. 'Yeah.'

I smiled: 'And what does Kim think?'

'Obviously, she isn't very keen.'

'So the way you decided that Kim was ready for toilet-training was listening to grandma?'

She nodded. 'I suppose so, yes, but then she has to start some time, doesn't she?'

'She does, but in my experience it pretty much only works when the little person is ready.'

'What if she's never ready?'

'I guess the other question is: what if she's not?'

We talked a bit more, and it became obvious that Mandy had succumbed to pressure from her mother. Grandparents are great, don't get me wrong. Grandparents are just the best thing if they are into the whole grandparent thing, but however much they are into it, they don't get to vote. Grandparents can advise, but they can't vote.

'So what have you tried?' I asked her.

'I make her sit on the toilet every morning after breakfast until she does something.'

'OK. How long does that take?'

'Sometimes 20 minutes. But she refuses to do number twos in the toilet. She'll wait until she gets off, and then she does it in her nappy.'

'What do you do then?'

'I make her sit on the toilet again.'

'But she's already done it by then.'

'I know, but I want her to learn.'

Hmmm.

I looked over at Kim, a cute wee blonde-haired thing wearing a Winnie the Pooh sweatshirt and blue jeans with pink fluffy bits at the bottom.

I pointed at Kim. 'That would pretty much make her Winnie the Pooh-less, wouldn't it?'

Mandy smiled. 'I guess so.'

'All right then. Would you like to know how you can instantly take all the stress out of toilet-training?'

She nodded enthusiastically. 'I would.'

I smiled. 'Give up.'

Where things went pear-shaped

Because of all the pressure, Mandy had pushed Kim into toilet-training when I didn't think Kim was quite ready. Because of that, it had quickly become a battle that was taking over their lives. All the fun had literally been flushed down the toilet.

The easiest way to end a battle is simply to stop fighting. This doesn't mean you let kids 'win', but it does mean you have to be smart about where you choose to make your stands. One of the worst places to make a stand is the losing side of a bowel motion.

What's normal?

There can be a huge age range in children's abilities as far as number ones and twos go. A good rule of thumb is that starting toilet-training under 20 months is pretty much a waste of time. Physiologically, your kids just can't control their bladder and bowel until some time after that. Some children can, but usually the 20-month mark is the minimum.

By age three, about two-thirds of kids will be dry during the day — but remember, this still means a third won't, which is obviously quite a lot. By age four, most of the rest will have got there, and the majority of the stragglers make it by five. It's also worth remembering that, on average, boys are a little bit slower than girls.

Most kids won't be dry at night until they've managed to be dry during the day. On average, kids get there around age four, but there are quite a few kids who are not dry at night until they're rounding the mark towards five. Even then, about 10% of kids will still be wetting the bed when they start school. A smaller percentage can go on having wet nights for several more years.

The big message here is that not everyone is toilet-trained at 18 months as some grandparents and other assorted well-meaning busy-bodies might tell you. My advice is to smile politely at these people and tell them that you're aiming to have your children out of nappies by high school.

All kids get there, but they get there in their own time and in their own way. The worst thing you can do is dive in with unrealistic expectations, because that will inevitably end in tears.

How to know when your child is ready

There are a few simple questions you can ask yourself and your child that will pretty much see you right. Here's a checklist you might want to use as a guide:

❖ Are they around the 20-month mark?

❖ Do they have the language skills? Can they tell you when their nappies are wet/dirty? Can they tell you what they want?

❖ Are they eating plenty of roughage and drinking plenty of water?

❖ Do they know when you're pleased?

❖ Can you get them excited about the idea of being toilet-trained?

❖ Can you be bothered? (If not, leave them in nappies for a bit longer and chill out for a while.)

❖ Are you prepared to give it a go, see if it works now, but to stop if it becomes a battle and try again later?

❖ Do you have carpet cleaner?

If the answers to the above questions — particularly the last two — are yes, then it might be time to have a go. If not, or if you're in doubt, wait a bit. The nice thing about nappies is that they mostly don't leak, and you don't have to race around looking for toilets all the time, or have your little ones peeing in someone's front garden because there are no toilets to be found.

Nappies can be stinky, but they also keep things nice and contained, and there's a certain degree of freedom that comes from that.

A three-step toilet-training plan

There are a gazillion different ways to toilet-train kids — this is one way of doing it. It's a little structured, which some people like and some don't. I like structure with parenting stuff, because for many parents a clear structure helps them to feel more confident and in control. Having said this, you should feel free to change steps to better fit your child and your home.

Step 1: Create motivation

One of the best ways to make kids feel like doing something is to tell them that they can't. If you want your little ones to sit on the toilet, then before you actually start, tell them they can't. I don't mean that you set them up to break a rule, but what you can do is tell them something like: 'Now just remember, you're allowed to go in and look at the toilet, but you can't sit on it yet. Toilets are for big boys, so you'll have to get bigger first, OK?' The way you make someone want to look inside a box is to tell them *not* to look inside it.

Next step in the motivation phase is to steadily build the toilet up as a fun place to be. You can start to put up pictures, tell toilet stories at bedtime, and cheer every time you pass the door. The aim is to make your toddler associate the littlest room in the house with the most fun there is to be had.

At the same time, you want to be building an association with wet/dirty nappies as being yucky. You want to be asking if they'd like the yucky old nappies changed. Make a face when you're cleaning up the number twos, and when the clean nappy is on tell them how much better that must feel.

The final step is the countdown. Get a calendar and mark a day when they will be big enough. Colour in each day and make a big fuss of the whole thing getting closer and closer.

Step 2: Train Teddy first

Children learn best through play, so you want to utilize this as part of your plan. The best way to do this is to get your little one to toilet-train their favourite soft toy. First we have to teach Teddy before we get a turn. Make it a game — make it fun. Get your wee one to ask Teddy if he needs to go to the toilet. If Teddy does, then help him to sit on a play toilet and make a big fuss when Teddy does his business. Every so often ask if Teddy needs to go. If they say no, just say good, and praise Teddy for knowing when he needs to go and when he doesn't.

If they say yes, then light up the fireworks. Again, we want to build up going to the toilet as being fun.

Step 3: Now it's Junior's turn

This is where the carpet cleaner comes in, because once Teddy has mastered the skill, it's Junior's turn. You are definitely going to want to do this at the weekend when all hands are on deck and you can make this the focus of the day.

The first thing is to make a big deal of the fact that the nappies are off. You might want to go shopping with Junior before the big day to choose the 'special underpants' they will wear when they're a big kid. When they put the underpants on, you make a big fuss over the fact that the yucky old nappies are off and the cool underpants are on.

We have a photograph of our little guy in his first pair of underpants looking as proud as a newly elected president (a good photograph for his 21st birthday party just by the bye, or perhaps to leak to the press when he becomes prime minister).

Next thing you do is give them plenty to drink, and then every two hours ask them if they want to go to the toilet. If you've done your job with the motivation stuff, then they are going to want to go.

If they don't want to sit on the toilet, don't fight but go back and refocus on the motivation issue first.

If they do produce something, make a gigantic fuss. Rewards are good. Positive attention is essential. I also recommend evil sweets as an effective bribe at this stage.

As things progress, you'll want to substitute other less evil rewards (like stickers for instance), but at the beginning there's nothing like the promise of the rush of sugar to induce a bit of motivation. Most little kids would sell their mother for an evil sweet.

Expect accidents and mess. If you have white carpets, this will be an anxious time. If accidents happen, don't get grumpy or naggy — just clean it up and move on. You can also use this as an excuse to go back and retrain Teddy to make sure the bear has the basic principles committed to memory.

Keep up with the drinks and the two-hour toilet breaks, and praise any forward movement, even if it's just a dribble.

As time goes on, they are going to get better at this. As they get better, you can start to space the rewards further and further apart.

The next phase is to move into encouraging them to take themselves off to the toilet when they feel they need to go. Obviously, the first time they have a completely solo effort you need to make a fuss big enough to shake the roof. At this point we call grandparents, aunties and uncles, and just about anyone who will listen so Junior can pass on the outstanding news.

If there's a mess — and there will be messes — don't panic. Don't get upset, and don't get mad. Little people take time to learn. Expect to do some cleaning and then you won't be disappointed. It will take time, but you'll get there.

The most important thing: make it fun

I can't stress this enough. Whatever you do, make it fun. If it turns into a battle, the best thing to do is stop, back off for a bit, and come back to it later.

There are a million different ways you can make toilet-training fun. If you're artistic, you can use big bits of cardboard to make your toilet look like a dinosaur, or a pony, or a truck. You can have special going-to-the-toilet music. You can sing a special toilet song to your little one:

We like to pee, we like to poo,
We like to sit like a kangaroo.
We like to be a big kid and get our business done,
We think that doing pee and poo is loads and loads of fun.

There are hours of fun to be had with toilets — you just have to be a little creative, and the magic will flow. If you make it a grinding, stressful misery, it won't work. If you make it a jolly good time for all, then it absolutely will happen.

Dry nights

Remember that you have to have dry days before you try for dry nights. This is kind of obvious, but not everyone gets that point. Once you have had dry days, then you can start.

Same principles apply: make it fun, build it up, and stack the deck with rewards just as you did in the previous stage. The first dry night gets something very special, as does the second, third, fourth, and fifth. After that, start to space out the rewards a bit. Make them work a bit harder.

> ➤ Establish a routine of going to the toilet last thing at night before bed, and then first thing in the morning when they wake up.

> ➤ I'm a fan of night waking as well. Before you go to bed, wake your little one up and take them to the toilet, then pop them back into bed. It's a lot easier to do than you think.

> ➤ If there are accidents, don't make a fuss or growl. Accidents happen. If you have a bad run, go back into nappies at night for a while then try again.

> ➤ The little person should also help to strip the bed — not do it all by themselves, but certainly help. You don't want to make this punitive or shaming; just as with any other mess

we make, we help tidy it up. As time goes on, little people are going to get sick of changing sheets and want to just go to the toilet. In our house we also made sure that, if we had a shower first thing in the morning because of a wet bed, it was very short and functional. There was no nice, long soak or play, because that can become reinforcing in itself. In and out is the key with wet-bed-in-the-morning showers.

➤ Dry nights will come — you just have to hang in and wait.

If you're having persistent problems, then it's best to start with a visit to your doctor. First make sure there are no physical reasons for the problem, then come back and deal with the behaviour. You may also need to get some specialist help with the behavioural aspects as well. If in doubt, go ask someone who knows about this stuff.

Fixing Kim

I told Mandy all of this, and she relaxed a bit. She'd been fighting Kim for months and was utterly sick of it. She was actually quite relieved that someone had given her permission to stop.

'So just wait then?' she asked.

I nodded. 'Yup. Have three months off, let the dust settle, then try again.'

Which is what she did.

They had a break for what ended up being closer to four months. During the last month, Mandy started to work just on the motivation issue. By the time they got to launch date, Kim was positively chomping at the bit. This time she was bursting to go — psychologically speaking anyway.

Mandy made a Barbie toilet (the mind boggles) and Kim absolutely loved it. This time there was no fighting or arguing. No stress and no pressure.

Mandy used the tactic of plenty of water and regular two-hourly pit stops, and pretty soon there was progress. Within two days of this fresh start, Kim had her first dry day. Within a month, she was dry at night.

Life is so much easier when people don't fight.

Toilet-training

Don't bother even thinking about starting until your little one is *at least* 20 months.

Whatever you do, don't rush it. Remember that all kids get there in their own time.

If you're not ready to start, then don't. Nappies aren't all bad.

Once you decide everyone is ready, then try the three-step approach:

1 Create motivation

2 Train Teddy first

3 Now it's Junior's turn.

Start with plenty of water and regular scheduled toilet breaks.

Reward success with positive attention and evil sweets.

With success, hand more of the responsibility over to Junior to initiate things.

Don't make it a battle. If it doesn't work, either try something else or stop and have another go later.

If you have problems, or you're concerned, get a doctor to look at the plumbing.

Dry nights will only happen after dry days.

Don't let them drink too much at night.

Toilet breaks before bed, wake them up when you go to bed, and then first thing in the morning.

Reward success.

If you're still having problems get some expert advice.

14

Jimmy Crapperpants and the bucket of consequences

New referral

Family details	Simone (38) and John (41), and Jimmy (5)
Presenting problem	Simone called because Jimmy keeps poohing his pants instead of going to the toilet. Only used to happen at home, but now is starting to happen at school as well.
Notes	Pretty sure this one is a case of 'You're not the boss of my bowel movements!'.

Children can be lovely, but sometimes they can be completely gross as well. This was one of those times.

'He just won't pooh in the toilet,' said Simone. John hadn't been able to come to the appointment because he couldn't get away from work. That was fine, because in the great majority of cases like this it is all about making a few simple changes rather than some big 'how do we all feel about each other' touchy-feely thing.

'How long has this been going on for?' I asked.

Simone looked a little defeated as she reflected back on their long battles with Jimmy's bowel control. 'Ever since we started toilet-training when he was about three.'

'Has he ever gone in the toilet?'

She thought for a moment. 'Maybe once or twice a month, but no more than that.'

'And does he do it in the toilet at school?'

'No, but up until lately he hasn't been doing it in his pants at school either. That's why I came to see you, actually — after we started having a few accidents at school. I'm just worried, because now he's getting older and other kids will notice the smell and I don't want him getting picked on or teased.'

I nodded, understanding completely. None of us wants our kid to be the one who gets called Jimmy Crapperpants at school. These were not small concerns at all.

'So what have you tried so far?'

It turned out that they'd tried everything they could possibly think of. They'd tried all kinds of dietary changes, they'd tried sticker charts, bribes, ignoring it, yelling, taking things away from him, sending him to bed early, drawing pictures . . . and just about everything else they could think of. They'd read lots of books and scoured the internet, but still nothing seemed to change things.

'And you've had him looked at by a paediatrician?' I asked. It's always important to rule out any physiological issues before we go on to behavioural approaches. I was pretty sure it was a behavioural thing, based on what Simone had told me so far, but it's always important to cover the bases first.

'Yes,' she said. 'He's fine, completely normal.'

'Good. Now tell me what happens at the moment when he does a wee brown monkey in his trousers.'

'Mostly he keeps playing as if nothing has happened. It doesn't seem to bother him at all.'

'And when you notice it, what do you do?'

'I usually just get him out of the dirty stuff and showered and changed again as quickly as I can. I don't want to make more of a fuss about it, because we've done that before and it doesn't help.'

I smiled. 'You've yelled a bit?'

She nodded, looking like she'd just confessed to the Thought Police.

'Don't worry too much about that,' I said. 'I've worked with lots and lots of parents over the years struggling with kids who refuse to pooh in the loo. Eventually, if you spend enough time knuckle-deep in the brown stuff, *everybody* yells.'

She smiled and looked relieved.

'Shall we get this sorted, then?'

'Please,' said Simone.

'Right. I just need to know one thing before we get started.'

'What is it?'

'Do you have a nice, big plastic bucket at home?'

Where things went pear-shaped

In Jimmy's case, the problem was all about motivation rather than ability. He was able to go in the toilet a couple of times a month, and until fairly recently he'd been able to keep himself from squeezing out wee brown monkeys in his pants at school. It seemed to me that the real problem was that Jimmy simply didn't care about poohing his pants. He probably did from time to time, but on an ongoing basis he appeared to have developed the ability to detach himself from the unpleasantness of it all and continue on as if nothing had happened.

Remember way back in Chapter 2 where I talked about not making their problem your problem? Well this is one of those times. At the moment it was far more Karen's problem than Jimmy's, so we had to shift the problem back where it belonged.

The power of the bucket

If you've got a wilful pooher, and that's what Jimmy clearly was, then you need to work on the motivation front. Generally speaking, there are two ways you can influence little people's motivation to do something. The first is to give them something nice when they do what you want — for example, you could give them some praise, a cuddle, or a pony. The other way is to assist them to experience unpleasant consequences when they do the thing you don't want. The most powerful and the quickest way to change behaviour is to cleverly combine the two, so that they're getting good stuff for being good, and bad stuff for being bad.

The unpleasant part of that equation is where the bucket and a scrubbing brush come in. Once we've ruled out any underlying medical reason, and established that there's nothing stressful or disturbing in the child's life which could be driving the behaviour, then it simply becomes a question of whether or not it's fair for the person who didn't make the mess to clean it up.

I don't think it is.

So what we do is we get the little person to scrub their own poohy pants, because, if you're going to lay the little brown monkey egg, then you need to be prepared to clean it up afterwards. It's important that this isn't done in an angry or demeaning way because the point is not to shame or belittle the little person. The point is simply to clean up the mess. It has long been my experience with little people that, once they have to start doing the really gross bits of the clean-up themselves, then they usually get motivated to deposit pooh in the toilet simply because it's easiest.

Fixing Jimmy

'So you really want me to make him clean it up?' Simone asked me.

'Yup.'

'Isn't that a bit mean?'

'Nope. It's only mean if you do it in a mean way. If you get all angry at him, or try to shame him as he's doing it, then absolutely that would be mean. But if you simply give him a bucket and a scrubbing brush and tell him that he's big enough to start cleaning it up himself now, then it isn't mean at all.'

'But that's pretty gross for a little boy.'

'It's pretty gross for you — and you aren't even the one who does it.'

She grinned. 'True.'

'The main thing is that you should get him to do it without getting angry or disappointed or anything like that. You don't have to pile any negative stuff on top, just let the pooh work its brown magic.'

'OK,' said Simone, who really had come to the end of her tether so far as pooh was concerned, 'I will.'

'There's only one other thing I'd suggest,' I said.

'What's that?'

'When you get him to scrub it, make him do it outside. We had a similar problem with one of my sons — and the first time we got him to scrub his poohy underpants, he suddenly started swinging them around his head.'

Simone burst out laughing.

'Yeah,' I said, 'it's funny from a distance, but at the time it looked like a shit hand grenade had exploded in our bathroom.'

'Not so funny,' said Simone, giggling.

'Yeah, actually it *is* still pretty funny.'

I called a week later, and it seemed that Jimmy had got off to a bit of a slow start. After asking about progress, I discovered Simone had simply been letting him dip his underpants in the bucket. I suggested that there ought to be some actual scrubbing. You don't have to get all Military Boarding School about it, you just have to let the little person get their hands dirty a few times and the inherent unpleasantness of the task will take care of the rest.

Sure enough, with that final adjustment, all it took was a few days of scrubbing and Jimmy made the surprising decision to start poohing in the toilet. He was a smart boy and wisely decided that, seeing as how someone had gone to all the trouble of inventing a toilet, he may as well use it.

The toilet refuser

First rule out any other reasons for refusing to pooh in the toilet. Your GP or paediatrician should be able to help with this.

Get a bucket and a scrubbing brush.

When they drop a wee brown monkey in their trousers, simply tell them that because they're not a little kid any more they have to clean it up for themselves.

Don't be angry or upset or disappointed.

In fact it's best to tell them that they shouldn't feel bad about it, that accidents happen, and that you're sure they'll get the hang of it soon.

Remember that it's not about trying to make them feel bad — it's just about making them clean up the mess.

Once it is cleaned up, praise them for doing a good job, and move on with the day.

Most importantly of all . . . make sure they scrub their wee underpants outside.

Naughty little boys and girls

This, more than any other thing we've talked about so far, is the thing that drives the great majority of parents barking mad: naughty little boys and girls.

In the pages that follow I'm going to give you everything you'll need to get the upper hand with naughty little boys and girls. The tools in these stories have worked on every kid I've ever seen — and, man oh man, have I seen some kids! If this stuff can work on all of them, it'll work with your little ones as well.

By the end of this section you'll have everything you need to be able to look at your own situation, figure out where things are going wrong, develop a simple plan to fix it, and pick the tools that will get the job done.

All that and some cool things to do with a microwave.

15

Directed attention:
the case of the baby hippo

NEW REFERRAL	
Family details	Chris (36) and Marie (37), and Sinead (3)
Presenting problem	Sinead throws major tantrums that will not stop for hours. She seems tireless once going, and nothing seems to stop her. Parents say they have tried everything.
Notes	She even sounded loud on the phone.

There is nothing as piercing as the shriek of a small child mid-tantrum. The sound can peel the membranes from the inside of your skull. That's the sound that makes childless people on airplanes turn and scowl at hapless parents trying desperately to get their little one to stop. (I scowl back at those people— if you can make a two-year-old sit still for hours when they're tired and bored, be my guest, otherwise shut the hell up and leave those poor parents alone.)

'Hi,' I said rather loudly as I walked out to the waiting room. A baby hippo was in the corner, howling. On the outside she looked like a fairly typical, albeit somewhat distraught, little girl. She was a skinny wee thing on the outside, but inside was all hippo. Anyone with ears could tell that.

The baby hippo would have crashed the plane. She had a howl that would have broken the wings off a 747, not because of vibrations or anything like that — no, the plane would have broken its own wings off to put itself out of its misery. Even a plummeting, wingless death would have been better than this living nightmare.

Her mother smiled apologetically at me. 'I'm sorry,' she said over the din. 'She wants to play with the pot plant.'

I waved a hand. 'No need to apologize,' I said. 'Howling children are what I do. We have special inserts in our ears so we don't get bothered by this stuff.' It wasn't true, but I made myself a mental note to investigate that idea further.

'We'd better reschedule the appointment,' said Marie, still looking apologetic.

'Why?' I shouted. 'Is she not well?'

Marie shook her head. 'No, she's not sick. It's just that when this starts up it won't stop for hours.'

'Oh.' I looked over at the baby hippo. Chris was talking to her and trying to distract her with a doll. The baby hippo was having none of it and kept batting the doll away. Chris, bless his soul, kept trying nonetheless.

'Can we make another time for next week?' Marie asked.

I looked back at her. She looked both embarrassed and defeated. Clearly this was a regular pattern.

'Look,' I said, quite loudly, 'would you be prepared to try an experiment?'

'What do you mean?'

I leaned forward so Marie could hear me. 'Would you like to see if we can get her to adjust the volume a little?'

Marie shook her head. 'She won't stop, seriously. She can do this for hours.'

I shrugged. 'What have we got to lose? I'm here, you're all here.' She looked uncertain.

'Look,' I said, or rather shouted, 'how about we make it interesting? If I can't get her to stop, I won't charge you; if I do, then you pay me four times my usual fee.'

Marie laughed. 'No way, you probably have all these secret psychologist things you can do to make her stop.'

I smiled. 'Of course I do. Why do you think I'm trying to con you into the bet?'

Marie sighed. 'OK, we'll stay.'

'Right then, let's get to work.' I called Chris over. We shook hands, and exchanged unnecessary apologies and the obligatory don't-worry-about-it replies. After that was done, I told them both to follow me. Chris immediately turned and went to pick up the baby hippo. I tapped him on the shoulder and shook my head. They both looked at me puzzled. 'Leave her there,' I said. 'When she's done, she'll follow along.'

'But . . .' Chris said, as if the idea was too confusing to even finish the sentence rebutting it.

I smiled, confident. 'Come on,' I said.

Meekly they followed along, glancing back over their shoulder. It was a short walk to the room, which was just around the corner from the waiting room, out of sight. Along the way I made sure the front door was locked. No one was getting out until this thing was done.

As we disappeared around the corner, the wailing escalated to the tantrum equivalent of a force five tornado. I could swear it felt like the air pressure dropped as she sucked in the atmosphere in great shuddering sobs. The windows seemed to bow inwards.

'Maybe we should go back,' said Marie.

I shook my head. 'She'll be fine. Besides, at least we know she's still breathing.'

Marie and Chris looked worried as the baby hippo continued to howl. It was impressive, I had to admit that. This was a girl who had learned how to maximize her relatively small lung space in ways that almost defied belief.

'When did all this start?' I asked, wanting to distract them from their obvious concern that the baby hippo might actually pop. I didn't think such things were possible, although the combination of decibels and distress rolling down the hallway did make even me wonder a little.

'She's always been hard work,' said Chris.

'Somehow that doesn't surprise me.'

It turned out that Chris wasn't over-dramatizing. Everything had been difficult: a bad pregnancy, characterized by endless morning sickness, a terrible birth, difficulties feeding, and then the behaviour stuff. As parents, these guys had run the gauntlet of almost every stressful thing. They were still struggling with getting her to eat, and sleep was a nightmare as well. Both Marie and Chris felt as if they were constantly on her case.

'All we ever seem to do is growl at her,' said Chris.

'Ye gods,' I said, 'I'm not surprised. How have you managed to stay sane?'

Marie looked at me, deadpan. 'You're assuming we have.'

'Good point.'

The thing that had brought them along to see me that day was an epiphany of sorts. Marie had been at the local park about a week before. The visit had started fine, but when Marie had told the baby hippo that she was too little to go down the big slide, the inevitable meltdown had occurred.

'I was standing there,' she said, 'with my daughter screaming and carrying on, thrashing on the ground and making a huge scene, and I realized that if something didn't change I would start to dislike her. I just knew that I couldn't spend the rest of my life with a child who behaved like this. I knew that I was beginning to resent her, to resent the way she behaves and how she makes me feel. I don't want to feel that way about my daughter,' Marie said, and promptly burst into tears.

I didn't panic as an untrained civilian might in such a situation, because — being a clinical psychologist with not one but two postgraduate qualifications in the intricacies of the psyche, years of experience working with the rawest edges of the human soul, and a deep and intuitive understanding of what a person needs in a moment of such unreserved fear and pain — I knew exactly what to do. I leaned forward: 'Tissue?'

Where things went pear-shaped

The truth is I knew as soon as I walked out into the waiting room what the problem was. You probably did, too. All children are piranhas, even baby hippos. Especially baby hippos. Marie and Chris had fallen into one of the single most common traps that all parents fall into: they were feeding the wrong stuff. The baby hippo had learned that the way to get attention was to perform, or rather in her case to shriek like the damned.

All their troubles, all the difficulties and heartache; it all came down to a simple little thing — they were paying too much attention to the wrong behaviours.

That's what I'd seen in the waiting room. The baby hippo was in full flight, and this was being rewarded with the utter and complete focus of mum and dad. She had clearly learned that the way to get attention was to create a mountain of stink. Things had simply spiralled out of control from there. It was no one's fault — this was just one of the treadmills parents often find themselves caught on.

God knows I'd run a few circuits on this one with my own kids.

The power of directed attention

There is nothing — and when I say nothing, I really do mean *nothing* — as powerful as parental attention. This more than any other thing can both explain most problems and fix them as well. But why should attention be so powerful?

The answer is that this stuff is in our bones. It's worth remembering that we're only 10,000 years out of the caves, a half-blink in the history of life on this planet. We share 99% of our genetic material with chimpanzees, although I've met some people over the years that I'm sure shared about 99.9% of their genetic material with chimps.

All of which means we're pretty much just bald monkeys with the ability to send text messages. Texting inane crap is obviously the reason why a prehensile thumb evolved in the first place. What else would you do with it? Despite all the trappings of civilization, our brains are still pretty much the leftovers of savages. We might sound very convincing talking to the man in the shop about WEGA televisions, but behind the schmoozing beats the heart and brain of a far less civilized beast.

In children, all behaviour is about proximity to the caregiver. When you're little, and fresh to the jungle, just about everything can eat you. I saw a clear demonstration of this one nice day when we took our kids to the local aviary to let the lads run off some steam. Our youngest son was looking at a rather splendid macaw (basically a very big and colourful parrot) when it let out a tremendous, ear-rattling squawk. My son stood there, ashen-faced for about a second and a half, and then he turned, bolted for me, and howled as if a tiger was on his tail.

It was one of those parenting moments when you feel sorry for the little guy, but it's also bloody funny at the same time. I took him back to the macaw and tried to broker peace, but he was having none of it. The point of all this was that my son obviously thought the parrot was going to eat him, cage notwithstanding, and his first thought was to bolt for the safest place available — me. This is instinctive stuff. It's in their bones. That's why anything that gets our attention is a powerful trigger for them. They want us close. They want us watching.

Who knows where the parrots might be hiding?

What this means, though, is that *anything* that gets attention will be labelled as good in their brains, and anything that doesn't will fall off the radar.

Ever done this? There are two kids sitting at the table, one is eating quietly, the other is splatting her spoon into her milk. The parent leans over, completely ignoring the quiet one, and instead blasts the splatterer: *'Don't do that Emily or you can go to your room.'* And of course, what does the good one learn? If you want to get your parent's attention, you splat your spoon in your milk.

Ever wondered why the little ones tend to pick up the older one's bad habits? Because *we* pay too much attention to the bad habits. If you pay attention to a bad habit, it will grow and grow and grow. Other little people will also want to copy it so they get the same kind of attention.

Paying attention to a bad habit is the same as voting. If you vote, all you do is encourage the politicians. If you pay attention to a bad behaviour, it too will soon want to run the country.

These are some of the ways we do this:

'Tarquin, stop that.'
'Why must you always do that, Tarquin?'
'Tarquin. Don't.'
'How many times have I told you, Tarquin . . .'
'Tarquin, this is your last warning . . .'
Tarquin, would you please stop tormenting that parrot . . .'
'Tarquin . . .'
'TARQUIN . . .'
'TAR-QUIN . . .'

It's painfully easy to pay too much attention to bad behaviours. The trouble is that bad behaviours cry out for our attention. There is nothing as irritating as a child bent on being irritating.

'It's like she does it to wind me up' is something I hear parents say a lot.

Duh!

Of *course* they do. They don't want to get us mad *per se* — all they really want is to *get* us. They'll get us happy if they can, but mad will do if that's all that's going. This doesn't mean you ignore everything. Obviously some behaviour you're going to need to step in with, and we'll talk about how to do this in the cases that follow, but a lot of them, probably 90%, can simply be ignored out of existence. If you stop feeding it, then it *will* disappear.

Usually when I tell parents this, I am met with a hail of yes-buts. The greatest of them all is the *yes-but-we've-tried-that-and-it-didn't-work*.

I have a yes-but of my own for that one: *Yes, but did you actually ignore it, and did you praise the behaviours you* do *want?*

When people say they've tried ignoring something, they usually mean they've tried to ignore it for about 10 minutes, then caved in. Or it means they ignored it sometimes and pounced on it other times. My position to that one is that, once you decide to ignore something, you ignore it. Forever. From that point onwards, the behaviour does not exist for you. The behaviour is a cue to disengage.

The little bald chimpanzees must learn that, when they start to grizzle, the momma and poppa chimpanzees drop the bananas and walk off. The wonderful thing is that because the little bald chimpanzee is so scared of being eaten by parrots, it will soon abandon grizzling and try to figure some new way of getting the big bald chimps to hang around.

Praise

Praise is the lifeblood of children. Praise is the holy grail of childhood. Once you understand this, you can fix almost any problem you're ever likely to strike. The thing about praise, though, is that the modern tendency is to throw it about like confetti. We tend to pile on praise for any old thing, and don't make too much of a distinction between doing something of note and pretty much just doing anything at all.

Some interesting research suggests that we can be a little smarter in how we use praise with kids. It seems that if you say 'You're very clever', then children tend to focus more on looking clever rather than on pushing themselves. Kids would rather play it safe and do the easy job so they can keep the 'clever' title, rather than push themselves to do something harder.

On the other hand, kids who are told they've 'worked really hard' seem to be far more likely to try to do better. For them it isn't about looking cool; it's about having the actual effort they put in praised.

So the big lesson here is: praise the effort, not the appearance. Instead of saying 'You're a good boy', say something like 'You tried really hard then — well done.'

This might seem like a fine hair to split, but if you think about it, it makes sense. Kids get showered with gratuitous amounts of praise these days simply for turning up. In many cases I think praise becomes a little like background noise. They hear it but it doesn't really mean anything, because they get so much of it for every tiny thing. Instead, maybe what we should do is target the praise to focus on actual *effort* rather than bland generalities.

I don't want to make too big a deal out of this, because it's a fair bet that Einstein's parents didn't think about the specifics of praise all that much and he still did OK. I'm just saying it's an interesting thing to think about.

I've summarized below some of the practical basics of how to give praise that works, remembering of course that effective praise is the kind that makes good behaviours grow.

The secrets of effective praise

➤ **Be specific** The technical term for this is *labelled praise*. This means you specifically describe the behaviours you are praising:

'Thanks for helping me carry in the groceries.' This helps children to associate the praise with the behaviours you want to grow.

➤ **Make it personal**   Use the word 'I' to make it clear that the specific good behaviour gets more attention from *you*, not just general good vibes from the world: '*I* really liked the way you went and got your pyjamas' versus 'Good boy for getting your pyjamas'.

➤ **Praise requires 100% focus**   OK, if not 100%, at least a convincing appearance of it. Don't deliver your praise over the top of the newspaper, or while you're staring at the telly, or from a different room.

➤ **Look and sound happy**   This might sound obvious, but a lot of people get it wrong. Just saying 'good girl' doesn't cut it. Words delivered in a monotone — or, worse still, in a slightly irritated tone because you're still annoyed about something they did five minutes ago — will not work. Look and sound as if you really mean what you are saying. Over the top is best.

➤ **Get physical**   Children blossom with physical affection. There is nothing so wonderful for little bald chimpanzees as having momma or poppa chimp pick out the ticks when they've done something good. This is as close to heaven as it gets. If you don't want to pick out the ticks, you could maybe give your kids a cuddle or a kiss instead.

➤ **Make it immediate and often**   You can't schedule in praise if you want to grow good behaviours. *Any* time you see *anything* positive, you leap on it with both boots on. The faster you tie in the praise to the good behaviour, the more powerful the message that this is a behaviour worth repeating. This means you have to make watching for good stuff a priority.

To complete the picture, what this all means is that the phrase you should have tacked inside your brain is:

Ignore the behaviours you don't want,
and praise the behaviours you do.

This is a very simple little catchphrase, but it is also a very important one. Once you understand how powerful the force of your attention is, then you have begun to master it. The purposeful application of your attention is the single greatest weapon that you have in the battle for world domination of your home. The trick is that you have to be the one pulling the strings.

Redirection

With little children, redirection is an equally powerful but often under-utilized tool for managing children's behaviour. Redirection is a wonderful tool because children are incredibly easy to redirect. They have very small attention spans as a general rule, and usually fairly short memories, so by simply refocusing them somewhere else you can almost always avoid the need for a fight. If you're good, you can avoid about 95% of the usual conflict just using redirection.

As I've mentioned earlier, the fantastic thing about little kids is that they also believe just about any old lie you tell them, which makes them an easy mark for redirection.

Another good thing about redirection is that it is playful and fun. In fact, redirection works best when it is playful. If it's fun for you, it'll work for them too. Fun is infectious. The limits of redirection are pretty much unknown. Every day there are parents out there pushing the boundaries of redirection in ways that were previously undreamt of.

Having said this, redirection is harder for some people than it is for others. They struggle with it. The truth is, however, that once you get into the swing of it the whole thing becomes easy and fun. For this reason I've included some ideas to get you started if you do find this stuff a bit hard.

Beginner's guide to effective redirection technique

➤ **Change the subject** This is the easiest one of all — simply change the subject. For example, if your little one is winding up about having a bath, simply change the subject: 'What did you do at preschool today?'

➤ **Refocus on a nicer part of the task** Instead of getting into a battle about something — 'You *will* get in the bath *now*' — simply refocus on a more fun aspect of it: 'I know, let's see if the rubber ducky can make bubbles.'

➤ **Find a more fun way to get there** Instead of being boring, live a little. For example instead of saying 'Come on, stop grizzling and let's go have a bath', you could say 'I know, let's fly to the bath like a dragon' whereupon you pick up your little one and fly them about the house, roaring like a dragon before landing in the bath to put the dragon fire out: 'Hissssssssssssss goes the steam.'

➤ **Just be an idiot** The silly stuff is always the best. You don't need to be especially creative, even. Simply let the idiocy happen. Just grab something and make it talk (such as a banana, a sock, a piece of wood). Or say random things that are all out of context: 'Guess what I saw today? A zebra walking down the road and singing.' Or do a silly dance together, or by yourself. Or teach them to hum on one leg. Or just about any stupid thing you can think of. Go wild — live a little.

➤ **The straight-out lie** These ones are good fun. As an example, in the middle of a developing grizzle, look up, go 'hush', and ask them in a theatrically hushed voice if they heard that sound. When they ask what sound, whisper very quietly 'Dinosaurs', then you both creep to the window to see if you can see them. Anything like this works. Ask a grumpy child in the supermarket if they can see the blue rabbit hopping about. All these things work a treat.

If you have a choice between fighting or chasing the blue bunny around the supermarket (collecting the groceries as you go just by the bye), it's often far easier and far more fun to chase the damn rabbit.

Fixing the baby hippo

Marie took the tissues.

I breathed a sigh of relief because there was no Plan B. What the hell do you do if tissues don't work?

She sniffled a bit, and Chris gave her comforting rubs on the shoulder.

'Well,' I said, after she'd regained her composure, 'at least there's one good thing.'

'What's that?' Marie asked, through teary eyes.

'At least the little one's stopped crying.'

Both of them looked at me in the silence which suddenly seemed huge. For a moment I thought they'd sit back and enjoy it, but anxiety set in.

'I'll just go check her,' Chris said, leaping to his feet.

I already knew that she was fine. In fact she was sitting just outside the open door of the room we were in, because I could see one little white stockinged leg poking out. I tried to warn Chris, but it was too late. She took one look at him and started to howl again.

I smiled.

I talked for about half an hour with Marie and Chris. The baby hippo stopped after about 15 minutes. The plan we developed was a very simple one. They were to simply ignore the bad behaviours, and praise the good ones.

To do this properly I had to be sure that they both were in agreement about which behaviours were which. A lot of parents get into trouble because they don't get this bit clear, and so they give the child mixed messages by ignoring a specific behaviour at some times and not at others. If anything, this is likely to actually *increase* the frequency of that behaviour. It even has a fancy name: variable interval reinforcement.

I call it simply not having your shit together.

In this case it was easy. Bad behaviours were grumbling, grizzling, and tantrums. Good behaviours were playing quietly, cuddles for mum and dad, and helping out with the task at hand. As an interim step, they were going to notice and praise *any* behaviour moving in that direction. Simply sitting quietly for a few seconds qualified as a praiseworthy behaviour. At this point I suggested that they needed to take anything they could get.

In addition, they were also going to use redirection as much as they could. My guess about the baby hippo was that she needed to get out of the rut she was in. Redirection was a good way to retrain her to think differently about how to get attention without performing. The other good thing about redirection is that it necessarily involves giving attention, which can also help to head off meltdowns.

I got them practising straight away. At one point, about five minutes after she'd stopped bellowing in the hallway, a teary, forlorn-looking wee baby-hippo face poked into the room.

'Marie,' I said, immediately passing the ball. 'Redirection and praise. Go.'

'Look at that,' Marie said, pointing over in the corner. 'It's a magic kiss bunny.'

Marie was a natural. At this point even I was intrigued, because so far as I knew there were no magic kiss-bunnies in the room.

The baby hippo looked over at the pile of toys in the corner, a forlorn finger trailing from a forlorn lip.

'That's very good looking,' said Marie.

There was no 'I' in the praise, but I wasn't splitting hairs at this point.

'Shall I help you to look?' Marie asked.

The baby hippo nodded.

Off they both went to the corner and started rummaging about. Sure enough, there was a kiss-bunny, and when found it duly rained kisses all over the baby hippo, who giggled loudly.

In that moment I knew they'd be fine. Once parents have the simple principles sorted out, things tend to flow on from there.

I rang them in a week to see how it was going.

'Much better,' said Marie. 'She's like a different little girl.'

'What do you think has made the difference?'

'We've been really disciplined about ignoring all the ratty stuff and praising good behaviour. Now the tantrums are over in a couple of minutes, and she's become much more affectionate as well.'

'Fantastic,' I said. 'Well done.'

'The best thing is that I actually enjoy spending time with her now, because I'm not always nagging her about being naughty. I just blank that stuff out and focus on the positive and she follows along.'

I saw them again a few months later to help sort out a few blips with toilet-training. They were all in a much better place. Best of all, there was no sign of the baby hippo. It had apparently moved out, leaving behind a bubbly shining wee thing called Sinead.

Don't you just love a happy ending?

Using directed attention to grow good behaviour

Decide which behaviours you don't want, and ignore them
– completely.

Decide which behaviours you do want, and praise them
every chance you get using the techniques we talked about
before. Most of all, make sure the praise is for specific
effort not bland generalities.

Make sure everyone is ignoring and praising the same
things. Mixed messages will just make things worse.

Wherever possible, redirect to avoid a fight.

If the behaviours are such that you can't ignore them, then
read the next chapter.

16

How to make time out and sticker charts actually *work*, and why you should never negotiate with a terrorist

	NEW REFERRAL
Family details	Adele (34) , and George (5) and Katey (3)
Presenting problem	George is causing all kinds of problems at home. Never does what he is told and makes everyone's lives a misery. Adele says she has tried everything but George refuses to give in.
Notes	Keep it simple, stupid.

There wasn't much American foreign policy under the George Dubya administration that I agreed with, but one of the places where George Bush Jnr and I did agree is that you should never negotiate with terrorists. This is a very dark road to start down indeed.

The George I was working with — five-year-old George — was

a terrorist of the first order. It was hard to tell what his particular political agenda was, but anarchy seemed to play a fairly big role in his particular ideology. Little George wasn't as interested in oil as big George, but he still made a fuss.

Adele looked completely ground down the first time I met her. It was hardly surprising. George's dad had walked out when Katey was six months old. The reason he gave Adele was that he supposedly 'couldn't handle it anymore'. Uh huh.

He left her with a toddler, a new baby, and a bunch of debts. Apart from one birthday card for George two years ago, they hadn't heard from him since.

And what was she supposed to do? Adele didn't have much choice. She had to handle it because the kids' father had simply walked off the job.

Dropkick, is what I think of him.

When you have kids, you don't get to quit. You can separate if that's best for everyone — and sometimes it really is — but you don't get to just quit. You don't just leave. If you do, you're a dropkick.

Things had been really tough with the kids. Katey was a good baby, but George was really upset when his dad left. That's when the tantrums and the angry non-compliance had started in earnest. George had quickly become a very angry young man. He refused to do almost anything that was asked of him, was rough with his little sister, and seemed intent on running completely amok.

'I think he needs a father figure,' Adele said as we sat talking. She'd said that she wanted to talk to me by herself first, so we'd left the kids in the waiting room.

I smiled. 'I probably can't help you on that front, but I might be able to help with the behaviour stuff.'

'Seriously, though,' she said, 'I do wonder if that isn't the problem.'

I shrugged. 'It could be part of it, for sure, but nothing is ever that simple. In my experience, the why questions are always complicated and convoluted. All we want is for you guys to be a bit happier, right?'

'Yeah.'

'OK then, let's get the kids in and get on with it.'

Adele went and got them. Katey trotted in as happy as a happy thing. George trailed behind with a scowl that looked like it could take the bow out of a rainbow until all you'd be left with is rain.

'Hey, Katey. Hey, George.'

Katey smiled. George harrumphed into a chair and immediately started picking at it.

'Don't do that please, George,' Adele said.

He ignored her.

'Don't do that please, George.'

Increased picking.

'George.'

Pick, pick, pick.

'George.'

Pick, pick, pick.

'George.'

He railed at her: *'WHAT?'*

I was somewhat taken aback by his angry response, but said nothing because I wanted to see how this one unfolded.

'Don't do that please.'

'Why?'

'Because I said so.'

'Why?'

'Because Mummy said, OK?'

Pick, pick, pick.

'George, if you don't stop that, Mummy is going to be very cross.'

And? I thought.

George apparently didn't give a hoot, because he kept picking away.

Adele looked at me as if to say *See what I mean?*

I did, but probably not in the way she meant.

Leaning forward, I put on my *I'm-the-boss-in-here* voice: 'Hey, George.'

He stopped picking and looked up. Little kids are always fairly compliant for grown-ups they don't know, which is why George stopped for me and not his mum.

'You like playing with cars?' I asked him.

He nodded.

'I got some cool ones out the front. How about you go play with those for a bit while I talk to your mum?'

He looked at me for a moment, weighing up his options. I gave him my best firm-but-friendly *don't-mess-with-me-little-man-because-I-will-win* smile. He got up and trundled out the door.

With kids it's all about psychology. You decide that you'll win, and you do.

Where things went pear-shaped

On the face of it, you might think this one is clouded with issues. Here we have a deserted mum with two kids, struggling with an angry little boy who was clearly deeply affected when his dropkick dad left. Maybe George has repressed grief?

Perhaps the boy in some way reminds mum of dad, and so she has this repressed hostility towards him? Maybe the boy's behaviour provides a focus for mum so that she doesn't have to deal with her own feelings about the separation? All these things are possible, and all of them still bring us back to the same point: that he's a little man who's behaving very badly.

Everyone wants to look for complicated answers to complicated behaviours. I strike this all the time, certainly from other professionals and often from parents as well. In my experience, focusing on the simpler issues is usually far more helpful.

In George's case I thought the problem was simply not enough fences, and not enough attention on the right behaviours. George was undoubtedly upset and disturbed by the sudden departure of his dad, and that could well be the thing which kicked all this off. The problem now was that he was in a negative cycle, and if he didn't get out quick the wheels would just start to spin faster and faster. This little guy was in desperate need of fences, because he needed something in the world that he could depend on and trust.

All behaviour is communication, but this doesn't necessarily mean that children are always trying to tell us complicated things. Usually kids are trying to tell us very simple things. I thought George was saying that he was sad, that he needed fences, and that he needed a more positive relationship with his mother. He needed to be reassured about where the lines were drawn.

I thought Adele was probably carrying around a bunch of her own stuff about the separation, and this was making her feel alternately anxious and guilty. She got bogged down in guilt when she needed to be active and take charge. I suspected that at the time of the separation she had probably — and quite reasonably — withdrawn into herself a bit, which meant George had acted out negatively to get her attention. Now they were stuck in a vicious cycle. On top of all this was the guilt which stopped Adele from taking charge in a strong way, so instead she engaged in an endless process of go-nowhere negotiation.

I thought George was simply asking for his mum.

Children need fences

Does this whole kids-need-fences thing sound familiar? If not, you should go back and read the stuff at the very beginning about fences. Some of the unhappiest kids I see are the ones who have no fences. Children hate this — it frightens them. It is confusing and unsettling.

But why then, you might ask, do they push the limits so much if they want the fences in the first place? Simple — because that's how they find out where the fences are. It is in the nature of children to go as far forward as they can. They want to see everything there is to see, they want to climb onto the roof, to put their fingers into holes, to run off in a crowded shopping mall. They have a rapidly developing brain which is busy trying to make sense of everything it can as quickly as it can before the parrots get it.

Learn, their little brain says. *Learn as if your life depends on it.*

At the same time they also need to know that someone really is watching out for the parrots. They need to know that they can go so far, but no further. The world can be a very scary place when you're little, so you need to know that there's someone who will pull you back if you go too far.

If children don't have fences their world is an unpredictable and scary place. Because of that, they run tirelessly forward until they do hit a fence. If you don't build fences for your children, then you're going to spend a lot of time chasing them.

It will get worse before it gets better

This an important point, and one you will need to remember: if you put any kind of behaviour management plan in place, then the bad behaviour will almost certainly get worse before it gets better.

Why? Because if children encounter a fence where previously there was none, they will shake it as hard as they can to see if they can move it or break it. If they do manage to move or break the fence, they will shake even harder the next time. If the fence remains solid, the shaking will stop. It might be noisy for a while, but it will stop.

If you build a fence, do not move it, or bend it, no matter what. Expect a period of increased bad behaviour, and on no account should you move, bend, or buckle.

Ask, tell, do

You must never negotiate with terrorists. Never.

If you start getting into long, circular negotiations with children, you're already on the outskirts of Crazytown. Negotiating endlessly with children will only lead to frustration, yelling, and bad behaviour.

The simple rules that I tell parents to use are the oldest ones in the behaviour management book:

1 *Ask* the child politely to do the required task.

2 If that doesn't work, then *tell* the child in a firm I'm-the-boss voice.

3 If they still don't comply, then you *do*.

Of course, what you actually *do* at step three will depend on the situation. In this chapter we're going to look at two options: time out for unacceptable behaviours or continued non-compliance, and how to use effective sticker charts effectively. I know that many parents feel they've used these tools, and that often they haven't worked, but I'm going to show you how you can use both techniques effectively, despite what your experiences may have been in the past.

Sticker charts: a blueprint for good behaviour

Many people find the whole idea of sticker charts pretty tedious. These are the same people who will tell you they've been there, done that, it didn't work. These are also usually the people who haven't grasped the bigger picture. They think sticker charts really are only just stickers on sheets of paper. As a result, they kind of do a chart for a bit, then they start to forget to put the stickers on, and then the whole thing eventually falls off and slides down the back of the fridge only to be found years later when they're moving house.

The fantastic thing about sticker charts is that they provide a clear structure which you can use as a blueprint for good behaviour. Used properly, they can provide you with an enormous amount of leverage to encourage the development of good behaviours and provide a way to punish the ones you don't like.

Secrets of effective sticker charts

➤ Each chart covers seven days, from Saturday to Friday.

➤ Each day is divided into seven two-hour blocks, as follows:

    Wake up   —   8.00 a.m.
    8.00 a.m.   —   10.00 a.m.
    10.00 a.m.   —   midday
    midday   —   2.00 p.m.
    2.00 p.m.   —   4.00 p.m.
    4.00 p.m.   —   6.00 p.m.
    6.00 p.m.   —   bedtime

➤ At the end of each two-hour period, if the behaviour has been good, your child gets to choose a cool sticker.

➤ Lower-level bad behaviour during the two-hour period immediately gets a sad face, while *really* bad behaviour gets a cross.

➤ Consistency is key. Be as consistent as you possibly can with putting the stickers on for the good stuff, and sad faces and crosses for the bad stuff.

➤ If your child gets five out of seven stickers in a day, they get a token.

➤ If they get even one cross in any of the squares for that day, they don't get a token.

➤ Tokens can be saved up and 'spent' on treats of differing values — one token might get them an extra story at night, and 10 tokens might get them a trip to a movie.

➤ If you involve your children in the process of coming up with new treats and placing a token value on them, they quickly become very engaged and motivated.

➤ Once children earn a token, it cannot be taken off them. If they earn it, they keep it no matter what.

➤ Tokens, like stickers, should be something cool. In our house we have 'jingles' which are tiny little bells bought from a craft store. They look and sound great.

➤ Make sure that you go back to the sticker chart at the end of each period and make a *big* fuss over the sticker — just like you make a big fuss over the token/jingle at the end of the day. In our house, jingles are things of magic and wonder. We crave them.

	MONDAY	TUESDAY	
Wake up — 8.00 a.m.	☺	☹	
8.00 a.m. — 10.00 a.m.	☹	✗✗	
10.00 a.m. — midday	☺	☹	
Midday — 2.00 p.m.	✗✗	☺	
2.00 p.m. — 4.00 p.m.	☺	☺	
4.00 p.m. — 6.00 p.m.	☺	✗✗	
6.00 p.m. — bedtime	☹	☹	

Some people prefer sticker charts which are very specific about the behaviours that get a sticker — for example, 'making bed' and 'brushing teeth'. I tend to favour the approach of simply awarding stickers for 'good behaviour' over a fixed two-hour period. The reason for this is that it allows you to be flexible during the day and get the maximum mileage out of each sticker.

For instance, instead of saying 'Melissa, for the *fifth* time can you *please* pick up your toys', you can say 'Melissa, if you haven't put your toys away by the time I get back, you won't be getting a sticker.'

It also gives you a way to interrupt a day that is threatening to spiral down the plughole: 'OK, Melissa, you've already got two sad faces, so if you want to get a jingle that means you have to be a really good girl for the rest of the day, and remember, you only need one more jingle and you have enough to go to the movies tomorrow.' The promise of the token can help to refocus a little mind that is wandering dangerously close to anarchy.

What you'll find is that if you use a sticker chart such as the one I've described, your little one will quickly become very motivated to get those stickers. In the curiously weird world of children, just the sticker alone can be reason enough to put your shoes away by the time momma counts to three.

The miracle of 1-2-3

If you can count to three, then you already have a powerful tool at the ready. The simple 1-2-3 count is a somewhat underrated miracle worker. As with anything, there is some technique involved, but it's minimal. The secret with the 1-2-3 count is all in the delivery: quiet, calm, and certain. You don't yell or scream, you simply give the condition and count to three:

'Jenny, can you pick up your shoes, please?'
'No.'

'Jenny, if you haven't picked up your shoes by the time I count to three, then I'm going to give you a sad face on your sticker chart.'
'But, **Mum** *...'*
'One.'
'Mum, in a minute—'
'Two.'
'But ... oh, OK then.'
Stomp, stomp, stomp.

If they comply before you get to three, then all is good. If they don't, then three means three, with all that three brings. If you get to three, apply the consequence *every single time*. The 1-2-3 count works only if they know that three means three. If they do know that, then two is usually where the action kicks in.

Again, the secret is in quiet, calm, certain delivery.

The good thing about the 1-2-3 count is that it provides the little people with a very finite period of time to exercise some choice about when they do the task (about three to five seconds usually) and it draws a clear line in the sand to help motivate that choice.

The microwave as behaviour management tool

This sounds like something very bad, but it's nothing like what you're thinking. Actually, this is an electronic version of the 1-2-3 count, but this method allows for a bit more time to complete a more involved task, such as drinking one's milk. The wonderful thing about microwaves is that they have a timer that beeps when it gets to zero. This gives you a fantastic escape from nagging, because all you have to do is set the timer, tell the child how long they've got, and then leave them to it. Sometimes with the little ones you can prompt them along to heighten the tension ('Oh no, only 60 seconds left ... 59, 58, 57, 56 ...').

We had an issue with getting dressed in the morning in our house. Some days it was taking an eternity and we fell into the trap of nagging. The problem is you can't ignore silly behaviour when you need something done in a set amount of time. The school bell waits for no one.

We solved this problem by telling our little man that he had five minutes to get dressed, that we were setting the timer, and if it beeped before he was dressed there would be a sad face on his sticker chart. Instant improvement.

We don't use it all the time, or it would simply become a new way to nag, but we do use it when there is a need for a little more focus and we don't want to get into a fight.

The secret is that they have to fear the consequences of getting beeped before the task is done. Again, sticker charts are wonderful because they give you a bargaining chip. Other consequences are fine too, though, if you don't do the sticker chart thing.

Time out: how to make it *work* this time

In the last case we talked about directed attention, but, as I pointed out, there are some things you can't ignore — such as hitting, rudeness, and breaking stuff. When these behaviours happen, you need to act decisively so the little person is left in no doubt that the boss does not approve.

Which is where time out comes in.

I can almost hear the groans from here: 'Not that tired old thing. We tried that and it didn't work. We're sick of time out — give us something new.'

Actually, I *am* going to give you something new, but that's for older kids (six to seven-plus) and it's in the next chapter, so rather than simply ignore time out let's look at how you can actually make it work.

The trick with time out is that the impact is highly individualized. How you do it will differ with different kids. What you have to do is decide how to adjust time out so that it works for your kids.

The principle governing the effective use of time out — and indeed any punishment — is this: *you must use a consequence that has meaning and it must be consistently applied*.

There has been a rather politically correct view of time out in recent years; namely, that it is not a punishment, but rather a chance to give the child time to cool down and think.

Yeah, right.

When my oldest boy was four I put him in time out and said (breaking all the rules): 'Right, now you sit in here quietly and think about how you can be a good boy when I let you out.'

He looked at me with a cool deliberation and replied: 'Well, *I'm* not going to *think* about *anything at all*.'

I laughed my arse off, which also broke all the rules.

Time out is punishment. It works best as a punishment. By this I mean it is a response you apply to a behaviour so that the little person will do the maths and decide that the behaviour simply isn't worth the result. Simple.

Indeed, even the word 'punishment' has become unfashionable in these politically correct times. Apparently, we should only talk about 'consequences', because that's all very positive and nice. Bollocks to all that.

Don't get me wrong — I have nothing against the word 'consequences', or against being positive and nice. Generally, being positive and nice is a very good thing, but I also have nothing against punishment. I think 'punishment' is a fine word and a fine concept.

To work, time out has to be something they don't like. It has to be a punishment. Sure they can cool down, sure they can think if they want, but mostly you just want them to stop. This is why you have to make sure that the consequence you apply has meaning to the child.

The reason time out works is not because kids do a bunch of

thinking — they don't do a lot of reasoning, because kids aren't reasonable — it works because they hate being in time out and want to do anything to avoid going back, even being good if they have to.

This doesn't mean you have to be nasty and put them in time out in a box with spiders in it under a bed, but you do have to ensure that it is devoid of any fun.

The other key point is that time out must be applied consistently. This means that you decide which behaviours warrant time out, and then every time you see those behaviours you act without hesitation. The little person must get firmly cemented in their heads the fact that every time they do the bad behaviour, they will go to time out.

Every single time.

There are a number of options for places you can use for time out, all with their own pros and cons.

❖ **Time out in a chair or in the corner**   I'm not a big fan of time out in the corner or sitting on a chair. This can be hard work if the child keeps getting up and then you have to keep putting them back. On the other hand, it drives some kids absolutely batty so can work a treat for them. Some kids find it unbearably unpleasant to have to sit in a room and not be part of things. You just have to make sure you don't interact with them while they're there.

❖ **Time out in a 'couch cage'**   For a while we used the ends of two couches pushed together at right angles in the corner of the room to make a soft 'cage' for time out. It worked really well for a while, because we didn't have to get sucked back into putting him back in the corner and so could ignore him and still be in the same room. The downside is that kids get bigger and can climb out after a while. The sense of triumph on a little face the first time they escape from a couch cage is quite something to see.

❖ **Time out in their room**   This can work well for some kids and not for others. If the fact they can't interact with you is what they hate the most, you'll be fine. If they're content playing with their toys, then it won't.

❖ **Time out in a boring room**   Toilets, bathrooms, and laundries are good for this. The good thing here is there's nothing to do in these places, so boredom does the work for you. Just do the obvious thing and make sure all the breakable stuff is out of the way and anything swallowable is locked away. A wee hint, though: if you do put them in the toilet for time out, remove the toilet roll first.

❖ **Time out in Africa**   Works very well, but it can be expensive. It's difficult to get them on the plane by themselves, they don't like getting all the vaccinations, and there's also a risk they could be eaten by wild animals. Use this one cautiously.

Secrets of effective time out

➤ Use the 'ask, tell, do' rule; 1-2-3 count; or microwave timer.

➤ Once you reach the *do* stage, you must act *immediately* and *decisively*. There is *no* further negotiation or conversation at this point.

➤ You must also be *consistent* as much as you possibly can. If the little person knows that *every single time* they behave in a certain way they'll go straight to time out, then they *will* eventually stop.

➤ Tell them *calmly* and *quietly* that they are now going to time out. Do *not* yell. Do *not* get angry. Be like a Buddhist monk taking a young apprentice monk to time out.

➤ Do *not* interact with your child on the way to time out. From the point you decide that the line has been crossed, they are already gone. The journey there is *not* an opportunity for lecturing.

➤ Choose the most effective place you can for time out, bearing in mind the different options discussed above.

➤ When they are in time out, there is *no* communication from you at all. When they're out, they're out. There is *no* shouting through doors, and *no* lecturing.

➤ The rule of thumb is one minute for every year of age. On a bad night you might lengthen that a bit if you need a break to get your head together. You would also lengthen it if they need time to calm down.

➤ If you do put them in a separate room, don't mess about holding the door closed. Go to the hardware store and get a bolt you can use to lock the door. You need to be able to put some distance between them and you, otherwise they'll still be getting attention, and you'll still be getting wound up.

➤ Once the time is up, they can come out. If they're banging on the door, wait for a lull then open the door and tell them they can now come out. You let them out *only* when they have calmed. If the tantrum is going on a bit, wait for even a *brief* lull, and then let them out.

➤ If they are in time out for non-compliance, politely make the request again. If they refuse, then straight back in they go. Repeat this as many times as necessary before they do the maths and buckle. Don't stop until they do what has been asked of them. Believe me, they *will* buckle first.

➤ When they do come out move on as quickly as possible. *Don't* lecture. The best way to move on is to find something to praise as soon as you can. Redirection is very good at this point.

Basically, you want a place to put them which is so devoid of fun that they'll do anything they can to avoid going back there. For some kids time out in the same room as you works wonders; for others a separate room works best.

I favour the separate, contained area approach, because it also means you get a break. There is nothing more draining than having to constantly place a child back in the corner. This also means you can end up getting wound up further by the performance. If they're in a separate room, you *both* get a chance to calm down.

The importance of structure and doing stuff

Children love structure — they just love it. I've outlined how you can get structure into your behaviour management plans, but the need for structure doesn't end there. Children need structure in their whole day.

If there is no rhythm in the family life, no routine, then you usually end up with aimless, niggly, grumpy kids, and parents who aren't much better.

This doesn't mean you have to write out a timetable for the whole day, divided up into six minute slots. (To be honest, if I woke up and the first thing I saw every morning was a timetable like that on the fridge, I'd shoot myself in the head. It would be a little depressing to have everything planned out so anally.) Instead, I'd suggest that you have a general routine that is easy to remember, especially at the weekends when the days can sometimes seem very long indeed. Get up and have breakfast, brush teeth, get ready, and then go do something. You don't have to go out and do expensive things either — just going for walk down to the local park can be a buzz for kids. If it's wet, go to the museum, or take a walk in the rain. Anything — just go and *do* something.

Bored children are naughty children.

You might not feel like it some days, but I guarantee that

if you make the effort and get out and do something the kids will be happier, and because of that so will you. Cabin fever is a terrible thing in children. It can reduce the sanest parent to a gibbering wreck in no time at all. This doesn't mean you have to become some nutty entertainment director, planning out every last minute of the day. Kids also need to learn how to entertain themselves. It is a good thing, though, to plan at least some stuff every day.

Get a basic routine.

Get off the couch and go do stuff.

Fixing George

The problem with little George was that he was rude, disrespectful, and non-compliant. George was a boy in need of fences and direction. George needed a little motivation to engage in better behaviours.

The first step was getting clear about the behaviours that were unacceptable and sorting these out into a tier, from the lesser ones which could be ignored, to the more serious ones which needed some heavier intervention. In this case, Adele decided she could ignore the grumpiness, some of the minor backchatting, and the tantrums. The behaviours she could not ignore were the non-compliance, the rudeness, and the physical aggression.

The behaviours she wanted to encourage were the times when he was helpful, when he did what he was told, and when he played gently and appropriately with his little sister.

To achieve this, we used the tools I outlined above. Adele set up a sticker chart to help with the structure, started using directed attention throughout the day, and set up the laundry as a time-out room for when the tantrums got too extreme or there was physical aggression.

I told Adele to expect that things would get worse before they got better. George was a stubborn wee soul, and he would undoubtedly test these new fences with all he had. As I said before, it's very common for children's bad behaviour to escalate when a new plan is put in place. Again, this is completely natural and is simply how children figure out where the fences are. You push as hard as you can to see if it will break. If it doesn't, you can relax and explore the ground inside the fence.

'Most of all,' I told her, 'you must be determined that from this day forward you will take no more crappy behaviour. You will not tolerate rudeness or disrespect. You also will not negotiate. You will ask once nicely, you will then tell firmly, then you will *do*.'

Adele nodded. 'Don't worry,' she said. 'I get it now.'

And she did.

What I am always surprised by is how quickly children change when they have a structure around them. Within three days, George was like a different boy. There were some initial blips, but not many. He was in time out a few times in the first two days, mostly for hitting and talking disrespectfully to his mother. He also had quite a few crosses and sad faces on his sticker chart, but on the third day he woke up and decided to play the game.

'He was like an angel,' Adele said. 'The whole day he kept asking me when he could have his next sticker, and at the end of the day when he got his first ribbon [Adele used little rainbow-coloured ribbons for tokens] he looked so proud I felt like crying.'

'Wonderful,' I said. 'Well done.'

'And that whole directed attention thing has been wonderful,' she said. 'I don't know why it never occurred to me that paying all that attention to the naughty behaviours was stupid.'

'And there's no more negotiation?'

'No. None. Every so often we compromise over something, but I make sure it really is a compromise and not me just giving in.'

'Very sensible,' I said. 'You don't need to make everything a battle.'

'I know.'

'So you're all happier?'

'Yes, much. We have a lot more cuddles now, and it feels like 90% of the stress has gone from the house.'

I told Adele I thought that was fantastic, and it was.

We didn't finish there. A while after that, I did talk with Adele more about how she could help George deal with the possibility of unresolved dad-issues. By then things were a lot better anyway. With the behaviours under control, they were able to focus on developing their relationship, and Adele in particular could focus more on making George feel safe and secure because she wasn't having to yell all the time. So far as I know, these guys are doing fine. All of which just goes to prove that one good mum can make up for a dropkick dad any day of the week.

Or vice versa for that matter.

Behaviour management at a glance:
sticker charts and time out

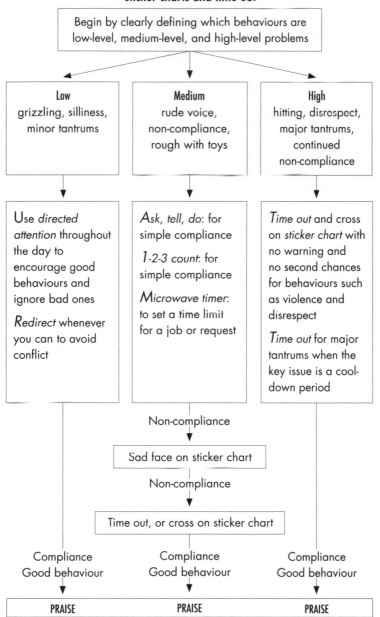

Begin by clearly defining which behaviours are low-level, medium-level, and high-level problems

Low
grizzling, silliness, minor tantrums

Medium
rude voice, non-compliance, rough with toys

High
hitting, disrespect, major tantrums, continued non-compliance

Use *directed attention* throughout the day to encourage good behaviours and ignore bad ones

Redirect whenever you can to avoid conflict

Ask, tell, do: for simple compliance

1-2-3 count: for simple compliance

Microwave timer: to set a time limit for a job or request

Time out and cross on *sticker chart* with no warning and no second chances for behaviours such as violence and disrespect

Time out for major tantrums when the key issue is a cool-down period

Non-compliance

Sad face on sticker chart

Non-compliance

Time out, or cross on sticker chart

Compliance
Good behaviour

Compliance
Good behaviour

Compliance
Good behaviour

PRAISE	PRAISE	PRAISE

17

The Ladder of Certain Doom

NEW REFERRAL	
Family details	Jack (46) and Jill (44), Oliver (10), Jamie (8), Samuel (6) and Georgia (4)
Presenting problem	Parents struggling to manage the children's behaviour. Jill said home is a 'lunatic asylum' and that no one listens. Fighting and yelling are the way they talk with each other. Things spinning out of control.
Notes	Sounds like everything is about to blow.

When I was a kid, the punishment I used to hate the most was being sent to bed early. I have a very clear memory of lying in my room one night — I must have been eight or nine — after being sent to bed early. I can't remember what I'd done, but I clearly remember lying there and feeling as if this was the worst, most frustrating thing in the world.

Years later, I was working with a family one afternoon and they were telling me how time out had never worked for them and no way would they try it again. I tried hard to sell it, but they just weren't buying. I sat back in my chair for a moment, stuck, and I thought back to my own childhood, trying to remember the punishments I'd hated the most. Which is when I remembered that night, lying in bed, and how much it sucked.

And just like that, inspiration hit me: *The Ladder of Certain Doom*.

I've used this technique for 20 years now, with all kinds of families and all kinds of kids, and it's bloody brilliant, even if I do say so myself. It's very simple to set up and use, and it can change households overnight. Results are quick, and they last.

Sound too good to be true? Well, read on.

Jack and Jill lived in a war zone. Their eyes had that look of people who don't live in the normal world. Sometimes you can just tell. It wasn't just them, though — it was the kids as well. The tension was huge, as though they lived their life permanently surrounded by tripwires. Little Georgia seemed blissfully unaware of it, but the three boys were dark and surly to a man. The attitude lifted off them in thin, sulphury wisps of smoke. This lot looked as if something was just about to blow.

I was almost afraid to ask a question — still, scaredy cats never prosper, so I leapt right in at the deep end. 'You guys look like a bunch of little unexploded bombs in baggy pants and T-shirts,' I said to the boys.

The two younger boys laughed, but 10-year-old Oliver shot me a look of utter scorn. His look said he wasn't about to be sucked in by any cheap little trick like that. He'd only just met me, yet he clearly felt entitled to act incredibly rudely to me. This told me some things about his world.

'D'you practise that at home?' I asked him.

'What?' he said, and this time he sneered — he actually *sneered*.

Oh my, I thought to myself, clicking into four-wheel-drive, *you and me are going to do the jitterbug, little man.* 'That little sneer thing you have going on there. That little . . .' I paused and sneered theatrically, '. . . that little hooky-lip thing. I mean, is that something you're actually doing on purpose, or is your lip just stuck on your tooth?'

Jamie laughed.

'Shut up, faggot,' snapped Oliver at his brother.

'Oliver,' Jack said, although there was a slightly hesitant tone, 'don't talk to your brother like that.'

'Well, he shouldn't be a faggot.'

'Oliver,' Jill broke in, 'just *leave it*.'

He mumbled something that I thought sounded like 'Shut up'.

'Excuse me?' I asked him.

He looked at me, attitude oozing from him by the bucket-load — all this in the space of less than a minute. 'What?'

'Did you just tell your mum to shut up?'

'So?'

I leaned forward, and dropped my voice just a notch: 'You know, Oliver,' I said. 'I only just met you and already I'm thinking you're a pretty rude young man, which is fine because I'm used to rude young men. I figure, as time goes by and we get to know each other better, we'll get to the bottom of that. For this reason I'll let your rudeness slide for now — not forever, but for now — but in my room no one, and I do mean *no one*, gets to be rude to their mother. So either you apologize to your mum, or you need to leave and go sit back out in the waiting room.'

I looked at him then, waiting. In such moments you commit absolutely. Me and Oliver were going head to head, and there was only one way this was going to turn out.

'I'm not gonna leave,' he said, although he sounded a bit more put-upon now.

I leaned forward in my chair and smiled: 'Oliver, you either apologize to your mum, or you and I are going to have a problem.'

Now, at one level I didn't have a lot to bargain with, because if he'd refused I couldn't actually pick him up and manhandle him out, much as I might have wanted to. Instead I simply wanted to convey to Oliver that *something* would happen. If *you* believe it, *they'll* believe it.

He turned to his mother and mumbled, grudgingly, 'Sorry.'
Good enough.
'Right then,' I said. 'Is this part of the problem?'
Jill nodded. 'I get this all the time.'
'He talks to you like that?'
She nodded. 'That and worse.'
'How do you deal with it at home?' I asked them.
'Yell,' said Jack. 'We yell a lot.'
It turned out this was a bit of an understatement. All they pretty much did was yell. Things had started to slip out of control. The children didn't listen, fought constantly, and were rude to their parents. Jill copped a lot more of it, because she was home more, but Jack didn't fare much better.

'Oliver just seems to hate us,' said Jack. 'I don't know why.'
Oliver rolled his eyes and harrumphed about in his chair. Still, he didn't mumble anything under his breath, so he'd at least learned not to do that in front of me.

'We've tried everything,' said Jill. 'We've used time out, taking things off him, removing privileges, everything. He just doesn't seem to care.'

'And what about the rest of them?' I asked.

Jill sighed. 'Now they're starting to pick up Oliver's bad habits as well.'

The rest of the children were also disrespectful and non-compliant it turned out, with Grace probably about the best of the bunch, although she was only four. She'd get there before long as well if something didn't change. Oliver seemed to be bearing the brunt of the blame for all this, but I didn't think that was entirely fair. Worse still, it looked like Oliver and his parents were setting themselves up for a very conflictual pattern just as he was heading into adolescence. This was not good. He'd need them in the years to come, so they needed to break out of this pattern now.

I did some preparatory detective work. It turned out that all the kids had televisions in their rooms, and the two older boys had their own PlayStations.

'What time do you get home from school?' I asked them all. About 3.30 p.m. usually. 'And what time do you usually go to bed?' The times ranged from 7.00 p.m. for the littlest up to 8.30 p.m. for Oliver.

'OK, now I need you guys to all skedaddle out while I talk about you to your mum and dad.'

Off they duly skedaddled — even Oliver.

'You two look exhausted,' I said after the kids had gone.

'We are,' said Jack. 'Our home is a horrible place, for us and the kids. All we ever do is yell at them.'

'We really need some help,' said Jill, and she really meant it.

'Right then,' I said. 'If I told you we could turn this thing around in 48 hours, 72 tops, would you be interested?'

They both looked at me, not believing but desperately wanting to. 'How?' asked Jack.

'You'll need some paper, a fridge magnet, a microwave, and about 20 minutes.'

They frowned.

'Let me tell you about the Ladder of Certain Doom,' I said.

Where things went pear-shaped

Jack and Jill had got themselves into a very common pattern. The behaviour difficulties had got everyone so wound up that things almost always ended in a screaming match. They were so fed up with the children's behaviour that they resorted to yelling as their main strategy. The kids, for their part, reacted to their parents being out of control by acting out more themselves. The whole thing was spiralling down into chaos: the kids' behaviour winds up the parents, who yell, and because the parents yell all the time the kids get more wound up so they misbehave more, which winds up the parents even further.

Jack and Jill needed a way to discipline the kids without all the yelling, arguments and stress. If something didn't change, there would be falling down, and broken crowns and much tumbling after for all concerned.

The Ladder of Certain Doom

First off, let me explain *how* the ladder works, then we can talk about *why* it works. Obviously the only prerequisite is that the kids need to be old enough to understand the concept of time. This will usually *not* work with kids younger than six. Even if your kids are older than six, you want to make sure they understand in a real sense the notion of time increasing and decreasing.

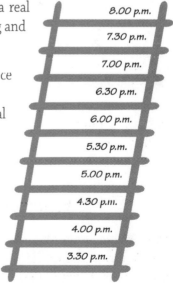

➤ Draw up a simple ladder on a piece of paper as shown right. The ladder starts at the child's normal bedtime and then goes down in half-hour steps until the time they get home from school. If kids are younger, you can make the steps 10 or 15 minutes.

➤ Put the ladder up on the fridge where everyone can see it.

➤ Place a fridge magnet at the very top of the chart. The magnet now becomes the 'flag' that tells us what time we're going to bed. Each child gets their own distinctive magnet or 'flag'.

➤ Every day starts with the flag at the top of the ladder — 8.00 p.m. in the example above.

➤ If there is bad behaviour, then the flag moves down a rung. If the bad behaviour doesn't stop in a given period of time (usually a 1-2-3 count), then the flag moves down another a rung.

➤ Similarly, if you ask the child to do a task within a set period of time (best measured with the microwave timer) and it isn't done, the flag moves down a rung.

➤ The flag keeps moving down until your request is complied with, or the flag reaches the current time, and then the child goes to bed. If the flag gets to 3.30 p.m. and it's 3.30 p.m., then off to bed we go.

This next bit is very important

➤ If the child has *lost* time off their bedtime they can *earn* their way back *up* the rungs by doing a *payback job* (see below).

➤ Really good days — when the child has not lost any time — are rewarded with special treats, as are really good weeks. You should decide what is a realistic number of good days to qualify for a weekly reward for your child (remember: it should be a bit of a stretch but definitely achievable). You might start with two good days and gradually increase this as behaviour improves. In this way, the ladder also doubles as a sticker chart.

Payback jobs

Payback jobs are fundamentally important to how the ladder works. Payback jobs are the vehicle for getting out of negative cycles and back into positive ones. The purpose of the payback job is to encourage children to enter into positive behaviour. Some examples of payback jobs are given below:

♣ sweeping the drive

♣ emptying the dishwasher

♣ hanging out the washing

♣ tidying up the room

♣ vacuuming

♣ doing something nice for the younger sibling you just hit.

It's important that children have a choice of which payback job they decide to do. Choice increases the chance of compliance. I suggest that parents have a small box of cards that children can choose from, each with a separate payback job written on it and the steps that each job entails. An example is shown below:

Emptying the dishwasher

1 Carefully take each piece out of the dishwasher.

2 Make sure it is dry.

3 Put it away in the right place.

4 Close the dishwasher.

5 Wipe away any water on the bench.

This might seem a bit pedantic, but if you don't you can end up in a debate about whether or not the job is finished. With the card, all you have to do is look at the card, look at what they've done, and then the answer is clear. If there's still water on the bench, you simply say: 'That's good, but you forgot step five. Tell me when it's done and I'll let you move the flag up.'

Obviously some jobs are bigger than others, and so you might get to go up two rungs (one hour) for cleaning your room, and only one rung (half an hour) for sweeping the drive. This will also depend on the age of the child.

On completion of the payback job, you lavish them with praise and make sure the little person feels good for making the decision to get off the grumpy train and climb back on board with the team.

'Yes, but my kids won't go to bed early, even if I tell them to'

This is the most common yes-but that I get when I tell parents about the Ladder of Certain Doom. Some parents — particularly where there has been a lot of yelling and out-of-control behaviour — are too scared to try this in case their kids refuse to go. Worse still, some parents are convinced they won't be able to get their kids to go to bed.

If you're feeling like that right now, then this is the best tool for you, because you need to regain control. Your kids have got the high ground at the moment. Your kids are directing the play. You do *not* want your children deciding what they will and will not do. This is a recipe for complete disaster. It *will* get worse if you don't take steps to regain control now.

There is only one approach possible here: you must commit absolutely to the fact that *you* will decide what your kids will and will not do. If you say they are going to bed now, then come hell or high water, they *will* go to bed now. If need be, you will physically pick the child up and carry them there, and you will sit outside the door all night if you have to. There is no other option but compliance. If the flag says bed, then *you* say bed, and they *go* to bed. Obviously no kid is going to stay in their actual bed from

3.30 p.m., but they can stay in their pyjamas, and they can stay in their room. They can still have dinner, but they have it in their room.

If your child was about to jump into a tank full of great white sharks, would you be able to stop them? My guess is yes. This is the same thing. You say, they do. If they don't, then you make them.

If they don't go, you can take things away from them. In fact, you can take everything away. You can strip their room of every last thing but the mattress, and not give those things back until you see some sustained compliance.

'Bed now' means bed now.

You have to remember that your child has no form of independent income, no form of independent transport, and no property rights. They have only what you give them. If you are determined, you can make that stubborn little person's life a desolate and boring place to be. Stick to your guns and they will do the maths.

Key ingredients for success

The crucial factor in determining how quickly the Ladder of Certain Doom works is how you apply it. The trick with this — and it's a very simple trick — is that you have to be like a machine. There's no argument, debate, or yelling. There's no emotion at all, in fact. There's simply the ladder. The responsibility for good behaviour rests solely with the child. It's not up to you to *make* them be good — you're just the one moving the flag up and down. If they choose to be good, so be it. If not, then off they go to bed. Once the ladder has been set in motion, and the rules established, then your *only* role is to move the flag. Gone are the days of nagging, debates, and multiple warnings.

Inevitability is the key here. If you have been caught up in all kinds of arguments and debates over behaviour, you simply stop.

You step away from all the heat and dust, and simply apply the tool.

You ask Jenny to stop screaming. If she doesn't, you tell her to stop, then if she still doesn't stop you move the flag down.

Easy.

If Jenny starts ranting at you about how that isn't fair then you simply say that she has until you count to three to stop nagging or you will move the flag down another rung.

Then you count: 'One, two, three.'

If she doesn't stop, you move the flag down, and you count again.

No arguments, no debates.

If you set a time limit for something to be done, then you put the microwave timer on, and forget about it. You don't nag, or remind, or threaten. If the timer goes off, you move the flag down a rung, and set it again, although for a shorter period this time. If the child comes wailing to you about how unfair it all is, you simply say: 'Don't argue with me, talk to the microwave.' Then you go back to reading the paper, ignoring all the wailing and protests until the timer beeps again. Then you move the flag down another rung, and set the timer again.

If the kids get the idea that there is nothing to argue against, and no way of stopping the flag, they *will* buckle and they *will* comply. If you're prepared to send your kids to bed at 3.30 p.m. every day for the rest of their lives, then I guarantee you won't have to do it more than about two or three times. The most stubborn kids I've worked with over the past 20 years haven't lasted more than four days when this thing is applied in a consistent, machine-like way.

Why does it work?

There are a number of reasons why such a simple tool works so effectively to reduce stress in families:

♣ It calms things down.

♣ It teaches self-responsibility.

♣ It teaches kids to manage their emotions.

♣ It radically increases the chances of getting back into a
positive cycle.

First, it gives parents a way to disengage from all the negative
emotion and to feel a detached sense of calm. There's no fighting
or yelling, no wrestling people to time out, or taking things away
from screaming kids. There's just a little flag that moves quietly
up and down. If parents are feeling calm and in control, they're
more able to effectively manage the situation.

The ladder also places the responsibility for behaviour squarely
on the shoulders of the child. There is no one to argue with,
nothing to fight against, nothing to kick or batter. They either
choose to calm themselves down, or they don't. Whatever choice
the little person makes, the consequences inevitably flow on from
their decision.

The ladder also teaches kids to manage their emotions. The
ability to self-soothe is an important skill to learn. Kids need to
be able to calm themselves down and think about where their
behaviour is leading them. The ladder makes this more likely
because their only way out of a negative cycle is to learn how
to chill out and make good choices. If they don't choose to calm
down, they have plenty of time to reflect on that decision when
they're in bed at 4.00 p.m.

Finally, the ladder provides a clear motivation for kids to get
into a positive cycle through the payback jobs. You don't have to
nag them to do a job — they do it if *they* choose, and they also do
the *job* they choose. If they don't want to do a payback job that's
up to them, but they don't get to climb back up the ladder. You
can't force a child to flip back into a positive mood, but you can
stack the dice to make it more likely.

Fixing Oliver, Jamie, Samuel and Georgia

I sat back in my chair, having just delivered my Ladder of Certain Doom spiel, and asked Jack and Jill what they thought.

'I like it,' said Jill.

Jack nodded. 'Me, too. It sounds good.'

'Great,' I said. 'So what you do now is go home, draw up the ladder, then sit down with the kids and explain how it's going to work. Then you set the thing in motion.'

'OK,' said Jill. 'We will.'

'But remember,' I said, 'you have to be like a machine with this thing. You set the conditions and then all you do is move the flag. There is no yelling, arguing, or nagging. You simply make a request and then pass it over to the ladder to deal with.'

Jack smiled. 'Oliver's going to be going to bed early until he's 20.'

'If you're prepared to follow through until he's 20, I'd predict you'll only have to do that twice at the most.'

Actually, Oliver was way smarter than that. His younger brother Jamie turned out to be the really stubborn one. Oliver went to bed an hour early on the first night; Jamie was in bed by 5 p.m. Next night, Oliver was in bed only a half-hour early; Jamie went at 4.30 p.m. Over the week, Oliver and the littlest brother, Samuel, were fine. Jamie, aged eight, took a bit longer, but he got there as well. Within seven days all three boys were getting special treats for days with no lost time. Oliver and Jamie slipped up a little now and then, but not much.

Little Georgia was too young for the ladder, so instead Jack and Jill used a combination of directed attention, distraction, and sticker charts, which worked just fine. Needless to say they employed the use of directed attention and distraction with the older kids as well.

I saw the family again two weeks later, and they were like different people. The tension seemed to have packed up and moved on to greener pastures. These guys looked positively relaxed. Even Oliver gave me a grudging smile when he walked in. I liked him — he was a cool kid. Stroppy, but definitely cool.

'It's like a miracle,' said Jill. 'Everything is just so much better. We don't yell and scream anymore. It's actually quite nice being at home now, isn't it Oliver?

He shrugged, but there was no edge to it this time.

We had another couple of sessions together, mostly focusing on the way they worked together as a family. In particular I wanted to make sure that Jack and Jill had the right skills to continue to build their relationships with all the children (using the tools I talked about in the section 'Inside little people's heads'), and to heal some of the emotional bruises from the bad old days.

One of the nicest things for them all was that, now they weren't all yelling at each other, they could spend more time doing fun things as a family. Jill and Jack could also spend more time focusing on talking with the children and doing all the things that make kids shine.

Shining kids are the best kind.

The Ladder of Certain Doom

If your home is marked by lots of yelling and negative emotions, use the Ladder of Certain Doom. This is an effective way to drain all the stress immediately and get compliance in a short period of time.

As always, be clear about which behaviours you want and which you don't want.

Remember that inevitability and lack of emotion are key.

Every day starts at the top of the ladder.

Ask, tell, do; use the 1-2-3 count; or the microwave timer.

Lose a half-hour for non-compliance or lower-level behaviours, and loss of an hour for higher-level behaviours such as aggression or disrespect.

Do not yell, argue or debate. Be like a robot. Warn, wait, then move the flag.

If they argue or protest excessively, give them a 1-2-3 count then move the flag.

When the flag says it's bedtime, then it's bedtime.

Give them the opportunity to do payback jobs to earn back time using the card system described earlier.

Reward a predetermined number of days where the flag either has not moved at all, or has moved only half an hour, with special treats or privileges.

The third drawer

Go to any kitchen in the world and you will invariably find that the third drawer down is always a surprise.

The first drawer is where you find the cutlery — knives, forks, spoons and teaspoons — all neatly laid out like little steel soldiers catching a nap in the trenches before the next big assault.

The second drawer tends to have the bigger stuff — carving knives, tin openers, wooden spoons, spatulas, sieves, bottle-openers, potato-peelers and corkscrews. This is all serious, sensible stuff.

But it's the third drawer down which is always a place of mystery and wonder. You never know what you're going to strike in the third drawer. It's like a whole other world of stuff which deserves to be there, but clearly doesn't fit in the first two drawers. You could find anything in the third drawer, anything at all. Maybe a set of fondue skewers, or a magnifying glass, or even a dinosaur key ring . . .

Mystery and wonder.

This section is that third drawer.

18

'Go outside and play'

When did it become our job to keep our kids entertained every moment of the night and day? I don't understand this at all, because I know that my parents' generation didn't feel the same pressure that my generation does to keep children entertained. Somehow, somewhere, the job got all that much more complicated.

I remember as a wee lad going to my father who was watching cricket on television and informing him that I was bored. I wasn't a great fan of the game, but my dad was a huge fan. He loved nothing more than sitting watching cricket for the day. The whole bloody day.

'Da-a-a-a-d?' I whined.

Nothing.

'Da-a-a-a-d?' I repeated.

My father leapt to his feet and bellowed out, 'Oh my God, what was that?'

I panicked for a moment, but then realized he wasn't talking to me: he was talking to the television, clearly under the impression that it was a two-way communication device and his heartfelt query would be passed on to the batsman.

'*Da-a-a-a-d?*' I whined again, louder this time, after he'd sat down.

He finally looked up and seemed surprised to see me standing there. 'What's up, mate?'

'I'm bored. Can we go out somewhere?'

'Nope. I'm watching the cricket: go outside and play.'

And the thing was he really meant it. He wasn't fooling around, he really wanted me to go outside and play. And what's more, fool that I was, that's exactly what I did.

Except the next bit is the weird bit, and it's the thing that, even all these years later, I still can't explain: nothing bad happened.

Weird, huh?

Not a single bad thing.

I didn't feel rejected, or unloved, or misunderstood. I didn't suffer from a lack of male role modelling, or generalized father issues. Not only that, but I didn't slip on the wet grass, poke my eye out with a stick, get eaten by polar bears, catch fire, or get struck down by swine flu. From memory, I think I just went outside and played in a hut we'd built in some trees up behind our house.

I think I even had fun.

I wouldn't want you to think that was all my dad ever did, because it wasn't. He was involved in my life in all kinds of ways, and I've got many happy memories of times we all went out and did family stuff. The difference is that he was quite clear that, despite the fact he was a parent, he was still entitled to spend the day yelling at people on television when they did something he thought was stupid.

Modern parenting seems to have fully embraced the idea that our job is to be the in-flight entertainment directors supplying them with an endless stream of stimulating and rewarding activities whenever they feel ill-at-ease, out of sorts, or lost for something to do. If they say they're bored, then all too often we're the ones down there building block towers, cutting out shapes, or helping paint pictures of dinosaurs.

I don't think it *is* our job to keep them entertained all the time. In fact, I think that — far from helping them out — we're actually cheating them out of a valuable learning experience. Boredom is a great provoker, it can be the first spark in a chain that begins on a rainy afternoon and ends in a pitched battle in the magical land of Morgoth against the dreaded Soul Monkey. Boredom can turn a previously non-descript box into a jet fighter, or a pony, or a robot. Boredom can be the shove that gets you out on that trampoline, or bike, or tree.

In any case, boredom is a part of life that they're going to have to come to terms with sooner or later. Large stretches of everyday life can be boring and so the ability to entertain yourself — or at least to endure it without causing irritation to others — is a skill they're going to need to have.

I'm not for a moment saying you shouldn't go out and spend time with your kids, because you absolutely should. Not only can these moments be terrific fun, but you also only ever get a limited amount of time to do that stuff. Before you know it, they'll be grown and gone and you'll be regretting you didn't do it more.

The important thing, though, is that you don't have to do that *all* the time. Have adventures, go for walks, build tree-houses if you have the equipment and aptitude for that stuff — just don't feel that you have to do it all the time or you're a bad parent.

Just this very afternoon my elder son came down to my office and informed me that he was bored.

'Really?' I said.

'Yeah.'

'Well, I've got this book to finish so . . . you know.'

'What's it about?' he asked.

'It's about raising kids.'

'Well,' he said, ever the player of angles, 'isn't it dumb to be writing a book about raising kids when you should be raising me?'

'Nope.'

'Why not?'

'Because I didn't sign a contract when I had you, but I did when

I promised my publisher I'd get this book done. Unless you've got a good lawyer, then I think the book comes first.'

He frowned. 'But I'm bored.'

'Good for you,' I said. 'I'm not, I'm busy. Go outside and play.'

'But—'

'Here's how it works,' I said, cutting in to what would have been a three-hour debate if I'd let him run on. 'I'm going to count to three, and if you aren't out of my office by the time I get to three, then I'll take half an hour off your bedtime.'

'But—'

'One . . .'

'Da-a-a-a-d.'

'Two . . .'

Click, which is of course the sound a door makes as it announces that a small boy is embarking on some grand new adventure.

Somehow I think my dad would approve.

19

Lies we tell our children

I'm a firm believer in lying to children, if for no other reason than it is fantastic fun. You see we all lie to our children, in all kinds of ways about all kinds of things. There's nothing wrong with this, because children have to learn the subtleties of lying so they can peacefully co-exist with others. If we couldn't lie, the world would be a disturbing, dysfunctional, dangerous place. Very few relationships could withstand the test of complete honesty. Consider for example that old chestnut: 'Does my bum look big in this?' How long would the fabric of civilization last if we had to answer that question honestly?

So no, there's nothing wrong with lying — which is just as well, because we do lie to our children an awful lot. Many of these lies are the ways we make childhood more magical. Things like the big fat guy in the red suit who comes and leaves presents, and the rabbit who leaves chocolate eggs.

Then there are the lies which seem quite magical, but on closer inspection are just bloody creepy. Perhaps the most glaring example is the tooth fairy. When you think that weird chick all the way through, it's enough to make you lose sleep. Somehow a lady dressed in a fairy costume creeps into the house in the dead of night — even though all the doors and windows are locked to stop people from breaking in and murdering us all in our beds — and she creeps about the house until she finds the dead tooth in the glass of water, by the small sleeping child, and she takes the tooth away with her to do God knows what sick shit with it, leaving money in its place. This is a woman who thinks a child's dead tooth is worth more than money. That's one sick lady, and one creepy lie.

Then of course there are the many and varied gratuitous lies that you can tell your kids simply to make your day more fun:

'Mum?'
'What?'
'Where are we going?'
'I've signed you all up at pirate school, so we have to go and
    get a parrot and an eyepatch for each of you.'

Or you can use lies as a rather clever technique for responding when you don't know the actual answer:

'Dad?'
'What?'
'Where do clouds come from?'
'From when sky monkeys fart.'

Or, as I did recently in this exchange with my six-year-old son, you can use a lie coupled with diversion to get yourself out of a conversation you're just not ready to have:

'Dad?'
'What?'
'How does the baby get out of Mum's tummy?'
A pause. 'On a motorbike, son. Would you like to go get
    an ice cream?'

In all these situations lies are helpful, and fun, and somehow just make the road a little easier. There are, however, lies we tell our kids that I don't think are helpful. In fact, I think these lies set kids up for disappointment and heartbreak. I don't tell my kids these lies, because I'd rather they knew the truth about this stuff.

So what are they?

Life is fair

Except of course that it isn't, not even a little bit. Most of the time life is pretty *unfair*. Good people get cancer, while bad people live to a ripe old age. Politicians start wars and then leave it up to us to go off and actually fight them. Rich Wall Street bankers act like greedy, reckless fools, and when it all falls over we lose our jobs, homes, and savings. George W Bush got not one term, but two. None of that is fair, not even a little bit.

Everyone gets a turn

No, they don't. It's been my turn for a few moments' peace and quiet for at least nine years, but it still hasn't come. Just like it's been my turn to ride in a private jet instead of cramped up in economy class. It's also been my turn to win the lottery for at least six years, but still it hasn't come.

You can do anything you want if you try hard enough

No, you can't. There are plenty of talented people who never make it, and plenty of talentless people who do. Why is it that some gifted musicians never get further than playing local pubs and some play stadiums? And why do some gifted leaders only ever lead their local sports club, and some with no leadership abilities at all end up leading the country? If you try hard, you are much more likely to get there without a doubt — but there's no guarantee.

It's not about winning, it's about taking part

It bloody *is* about winning. It just *is*. Taking part is great, and it's an achievement in itself, but it isn't quite as good as winning. Kids like to compete, and they like to win. If you look at anyone

222

who has achieved something substantial in life — whether it be in business, sport, the arts, or reality television — one of the core traits all of those people will share is the desire to be really good at what they do, the desire to succeed, to win.

Everyone gets a prize

No, they don't. In any case, in most things in life once you hit the adult world it's far better to be the winner, because in the grown-up world there aren't often prizes for second place. If you lose the big contract, you don't get a silver medal — you get nothing. There's good which comes from losing as well, because losing hurts. It isn't nice. Losing is what makes you either want to try harder or accept the fact that you're never going to be very good at something and make you go try something else you might actually be good at.

You're special

No, you're not. I don't mean that in a mean way, but the truth is we can't all be special. We're special to the people we love, and the people who love us, but we're not special in the eyes of the world. Some people are special — rock stars, brilliant scientists, artists, great humanitarians, Morris dancers and the like — but the rest of us are just average. We go about our lives buying toilet paper and paying our taxes and doing what normal people do. There's nothing wrong with that, in fact I think there's a great comfort to be found in it. When you really think about it, who would actually want to be a rock star anyway?

That might all sound a bit grim, but I don't think it is. I don't want my boys to grow up thinking that life is fair, or that everyone gets a turn, or that the world thinks they are inherently special. Life is none of these things, and the world simply does not work that way. If you think it is, then you're going to be disappointed, unhappy, and bitter much of the time. The world doesn't give a monkey's about my boys. It doesn't hate them, either; it simply doesn't care about them one way or the other. If they're going to be 'special' in the eyes of the world, then they have to actually *do* something to be special.

The last thing I want is for my boys to get out the end of childhood expecting the world to serve up a happy life to them on a silver platter, because it doesn't work that way. Once you get that life isn't fair, that sometimes bad things happen to good people, and that if you want stuff you have to go out and get it yourself, then you're more likely to actually get the kind of life you want.

20

How to be the kind of parent teachers like

It's really easy to be the kind of parent teachers like. And it's really important. Imagine, for example, just before first class two mums come to drop off their kids for school. The first mum smiles at the teacher, says hello, and then exits. The second mum smiles, says hello, and then traps the teacher in a long, tedious, and accusatory discussion about why her daughter isn't in the top reading group when she is clearly reading at a level that is far above that of her classmates. Which kid do you think is going to get the broken crayons in art classes?

Teachers have to put up with a lot of crazy stuff from parents these days, and they mostly do it with great patience and grace. I think that it would be fair to say, though, that there isn't a teacher in the Western world who isn't at least a bit fed up with some of the nonsense they have to endure at the hands of generally well-meaning, but often ridiculously over-involved parents. Here are just a few examples of the mad stuff teachers have told me they have to deal with now:

❖ A mother in tears because her six-year-old daughter didn't get into the 'advanced' art class.

❖ A parent who approached a principal wanting the next term's syllabus so they could get a jump-start on it during the holidays.

❖ A father who was outraged because his son was made to sit outside the staff room at lunchtime when 'all' the boy had done was tell the teacher to shut up.

❖ A parent whose response to repeated angry/disrespectful outbursts from their child in class was that the boy 'wasn't being stimulated enough' by the classroom teacher.

❖ A principal had to endure an outraged blast from a parent whose daughter had lost a game of tennis at lunchtime after the other children changed the rules mid-game.

❖ A parent complained that their child was being unfairly disadvantaged by having to sit at the back of the class, furthest away from the board.

❖ A parent who engaged a lawyer to appeal the decision of a school talent quest which went against his daughter.

❖ Complaints from several parents after a teacher told off some boys for yelling. The teacher allegedly 'raised her voice' which the parents thought was inappropriate.

❖ A parent complained after being 'told off' by their child's teacher for getting to school an hour late every day. The parent didn't think the teacher had any right to tell them what time their child should be at school.

Now, I could go on, but you probably get the point from even this brief list of examples. For some reason some parents of today believe that children always tell the truth and teachers always lie, and if anything goes wrong at school it's the school's fault.

Teachers don't like whiney, anxious parents. They just don't. They may well act as if they are listening to Sarah's mother as she angrily points out that Sarah never behaves that way at home because she is always stimulated appropriately, but inside they will simply be thinking unkind thoughts about Sarah's mum, and making a mental note to give the girl the broken crayons next time.

Apart from the whole crayons thing, the other reason it's good to have a strong relationship with your child's teacher is that if there is a problem they will often be your best ally. You don't want them to roll their eyes when they see you coming — you want them to look up and smile.

So how do you be the kind of parent teachers like?

➤ Don't make a fuss about every little thing

It's a simple thing, but important. Teachers are busy people, and schools can be a bit chaotic at the best of times. Sometimes stuff doesn't get done, and sometimes things are less than perfect. Be forgiving and understanding and don't complain about every last little thing. If you don't, they will be much more likely to take you seriously when you do need to talk to them about something important.

➤ Take responsibility for problems with your child

If your little one has got into trouble for something, make sure you get the message across loud and clear that you are taking the matter seriously, and want to get it sorted. It isn't the school's problem, after all — it's yours. We all want our kids to blend in with the school community and go about the business of getting educated. If there *are* problems, we need to make sure we're on to it as soon as we can.

➤ Work with the school, not against it

You'd be surprised how many parents end up in fights with their school over things which shouldn't have been fights at all. If you're practising the previous step, you'll find this one much easier as well. Basically, you need to sit down with the teacher if there's a problem and work with them to get it solved. If you approach any problems with the philosophy that you're part of a team, and the teacher gets the fact you aren't out to blame them, then most of the time most problems can be resolved.

It really is that simple. From time to time there might be things you disagree with, but my advice is pick the big ones and don't worry about the little stuff. Obviously, if you're really concerned or upset about something that you feel is important, you absolutely should go in and talk with the school about whatever it is you're worried about. If, on the other hand, you constantly feel as if everything is important and everything necessitates a sit-down meeting with the teacher and/or principal, the odds are you're probably getting a bit too worked up about things, and should take a breath and a step back.

After all, who wants their kid to be the one with the broken crayons? Where's the dignity in that?

21

Keeping kids safe

All parents worry about their kids — it comes with the territory. I have no desire to make parents worry more, so please rest assured that the world is generally a safe place, and that most people are good.

Indeed, if anyone had a reason to be paranoid it would be me. Alongside all the years I've spent working with kids and families, I've also been working with child abusers and their victims. I've seen every bad thing that can happen to a little person, and I've sat and talked with all the bad men who do those things. The bogeyman is not just a sound-bite on television for me. I know his many names, where he lives, and even what he smells like.

So if ever there was a person with a justification for being paranoid and over-protective, it would definitely be me. Yet I am none of those things. I let my elder son walk to school by himself, and the little one will, too, once we've got a bit more confidence in his road-crossing skills. They both go to friends' houses to play, engage in hazardous outdoor pursuits, own pocket knives, and jump off high things at my direction; next year they'll be starting soccer, and probably a few other things as well. My younger son even went to a preschool with — horror of horrors — a *male* preschool teacher. I take them out into the world and, despite making an honest attempt, never quite manage to have them both in my line of vision all the time. Sometimes, as we're walking along the beach on a Saturday morning, they even talk to strange old men walking stranger-looking old dogs.

In these safety-obsessed times it's easy to get swept away in all the carrying-on until you get to the point where your kids are barely allowed to breathe. We had those little plastic plug-guard protector things in our house, but every time I looked at them I felt like I'd been duped. Somehow my parents had managed to get four kids all the way through their childhood alive without the benefit of a single one of those things. Plus when you go to plug the vacuum cleaner in, they're a pain in the arse to get out.

So don't worry too much, because most of the time things turn out OK. To nudge this process along a little, I'm going to give you a few basic tips — my essential, practical, non-paranoid guide to keeping kids safe. It's probably good to think about this stuff, just don't think about it too much. Don't lose sleep over it is what I'm saying.

Relationship is key

In the chapter on talking with children, I outlined some basic tips for communicating more effectively with your kids. This applies here with boots on. The most important thing you can do to keep your kids safe is to make them feel that they can come and talk to you about anything, and that you will actually listen. You start doing this from day one, and it doesn't stop until they put you in a box.

Your kids need to feel confident that when they come to you, you will listen and help them to deal with whatever is going on that they're worried about. The more you know about them — their likes and dislikes, their friends, their interests — the more you are able to head off trouble. If you don't really take much notice of your kids because you're too busy, then you probably won't notice when something changes.

Listen to your kids

Building from the previous point, it's important to actually *listen* to any worries your kids might bring to you. Sometimes they can have a real big problem, but it's presented in a very low-key way. If your kids show a reluctance to visit particular people, or go to particular places, spend a little time finding out what that's about.

Similarly, if your previously happy child suddenly doesn't want to go to school, or starts getting in trouble at school, find out what *that* is about. All behaviour is communication, and so if you suddenly strike some new behaviour, it may be your child's way of telling you that something is going on that they don't like.

Listen to your gut

Bad guys very rarely look like what you'd expect. In fact, over the course of the past 20 years working with sexual offenders, only a handful of them actually looked the part. The rest of them looked like anyone you'd sit next to on the bus, or talk to at the bank, or even sleep next to at night.

For this reason you should always trust your gut feeling. If you have a little niggling doubt about someone or something, listen to it. Take whatever steps you need to take to ensure that your kids are OK.

If you don't really trust someone, then don't.

Always remember, too, that the stranger-danger thing is only a small part of sexual offending against children. The great majority of kids are hurt by people they know. This doesn't mean that you turn into some kind of paranoid freak and suspect everybody — indeed if you do suspect everybody, then you probably need to go get some professional help for yourself — but you should listen to niggling feelings. If in doubt, trust your gut, and not what other people say.

Be involved in your child's life

Tempting as it might sometimes be to let other people (such as teachers, after-school programmes, tutors, nannies, and babysitters) raise your child, it's probably a good idea to be involved in at least some parts of their upbringing. This doesn't mean that you justify becoming an over-involved obsessive nut of a parent by saying that you're just keeping your kids safe, but it is good to be in there to varying degrees. It's a delicate balance between fostering growing autonomy and being a passive parent.

Just do the best you can.

Ask

This one is painfully simple: you just ask. Find a quiet moment, a nice positive moment, maybe sitting on a rock at the beach, or curled up together on the couch watching a movie, and ask:

'Are you happy, little man?'
'Do you have any worries at the moment?'

It doesn't have to be a big intrusive thing — low key and laid back is best — but you can simply ask. If your wee one says they're happy and have no worries, give them a hug and say good. You could maybe ask them who they'd talk to if they did have any worries, and hope that they say you. If they do, all fine and good. If they say they don't know, point out that they can always come and talk to you, because that's what parents do — they help kids deal with worries.

Low key. Laid back. No stress.

Teach them to listen to their alarm bell

I've been involved in a lot of 'keeping safe' education with kids over the years, and I favour a fairly generic approach to it all. I don't like the idea of little kids coming up with a plan of what they would do if a stranger touched their penis or vagina. This always seemed a little too intense for my liking.

Instead what I do is teach kids that they have an 'alarm bell' inside them that can help them figure out if something is OK or not. It's such a simple thing even very little kids, four- to five-year-olds, get it straight away. If you ask a kid 'Would your alarm bell ring if a fluffy kitten sat down beside you?', most would say no. If you ask if their alarm bell would ring if a shark sat down beside them, most yell 'yes' at the top of their lungs. Similarly, you can pose a bunch of scenarios and ask them if their alarm bell would ring:

❖ An older kid pushes them over at school.

❖ A teacher does reading with them.

❖ A cuddle from mum or dad.

❖ A lick from the family dog.

❖ A stranger asks them questions.

❖ A stranger asks them to come over to his car.

❖ A friend at school asks them to help take someone else's playlunch.

❖ A friend gives them a hug.

❖ Someone at school asked them to pull down their pants.

❖ Someone gives them a hug they don't like.

❖ Someone gives them a sloppy kiss.

❖ Someone asks them not to tell mum or dad something.

These are all scenarios you can put to children using the alarm bell framework. You can also chop and change examples so that you can put some funny ones in to lighten the mood a little if need be.

'What do you do if your alarm bell rings?'

If their alarm bell rings, they should find an adult they trust and tell them what has happened. If they're at school, they should tell their teacher or any other teacher they can see. If they're by themselves, they should look for a shop they can go into, and ask the shopkeeper to get mum or dad. Most of all, they need to tell mum and dad, because mum and dad will *always* know what to do. It doesn't matter what the problem is, or how big it is, they should tell mum or dad.

It's also important to get children to practise what they would say. The way you do this is you simply ask them: 'If someone at school said or did something you didn't like and your alarm bell went off, what would you do?'

'Tell a teacher.'
'Good girl. Which teacher?'
'My teacher.'
'Fantastic. And if she isn't there?'
'The teacher in the playground.'
'Excellent. And what would you say?'
'I'd say my alarm bell just went off.'
'And what else would you tell them?'
'Ummm . . . I don't know.'
'You tell them what happened that you didn't like, and you ask if they can help you.'
'Oh yeah.'
'So what do you tell them?'
'I tell them what happened and ask them to help me.'
'Excellent. Very good. That's exactly right. And who else would you tell?'
'You.'
Hugs, etc. *'That's right, because what's my job?'*
'To help me with my problems.'

It's important that you rehearse with children what they would say. Often children know something is wrong, but they don't have the words to describe it. With the alarm bell technique, they don't have to describe the act to bring it to someone's attention. All they need to do is signal that their alarm bell has gone off and then let the adults sort out the problem.

'What do I do if my child comes to me and says their alarm bell has gone off?'

The most important thing is that you give them your instant and undivided attention. You want to signal to the little person that you are taking what they are saying very seriously. You want them to get the message loud and clear that if they come to you with a ringing alarm bell, you're going to be dropping everything to help them.

You also want to be calm and not panic, whatever the reason for the ringing bells. Little people need to know that the big people are in charge and always know exactly what to do.

If you want to freak out, do that later in private.

The alarm bell might be ringing because of something trivial today ('Dad, Jordan called me a fart pie'), but you want to have the drill in place in case they ever come to you with something more serious ('Dad, Jordan asked me to marry him and we're dropping out of school to become wandering poets').

Places you can go for help

If your child ever talks to you about really serious stuff, such as abuse, then you are going to want to seek out some more experienced help. The simplest and best thing to do is to telephone someone. There are many different places you can ring for advice, ranging from government organizations to private providers.

Most places and people who work with children in any capacity — from public agencies to private practitioners — are very helpful at steering people in the right direction. If you aren't sure who to ring, just get out your phone book, pick something that looks close, and ring them. If they're not the right organization or person to speak to, they will almost certainly know whom you should be speaking to.

The most important thing is not to feel as if you should know who or where to ring exactly. Just pick something close and you'll eventually end up in the right place. Remember that all the people in this game are there to help kids and families, so we don't mind if people ring and we're not the right place. If you haven't rung the right place, we'll give you the number of the right place.

Some guidelines for choosing the right daycare/preschool

Let me be very clear at the beginning of this that the points which follow are simply my personal opinion. Having said that, I have worked for over 20 years with all kinds of criminals, of all ages and genders and hair colours, including literally thousands of sexual offenders and their victims. It's an opinion, to be sure, but I'd like to think it's a reasonably informed one.

Some of the things I'm about to say will probably upset some people. I'm sorry about that, but these are the rules we've followed with our kids, and the advice I give to my friends. I'll give the same to you and you can make of it what you will.

➤ Daycare centres are safer than home-based care

I have never been a fan of home-based care. The predominant reason for this is that there is almost no monitoring of what goes on in the home-based carer's house. I know that there are many excellent home-based carers who do a fantastic job. My issue is not with them. My issue is with the bad ones. If you have only one person looking after your child, then who watches them?

Also, who watches the people they go and visit during the day, or the people who come to visit them?

If your child is in home-based care, you have no control or monitoring over the people your children are exposed to during the day. None.

In a daycare centre, you have a number of staff who effectively monitor each other, and hopefully there are strict rules about who is and isn't allowed to visit the centre. Again, you also have many eyes monitoring the activities of any visitors.

➤ Check the physical environment

Some of this is obvious, like checking for dangerous stuff lying about, but some isn't. One of the most important things I always look at is the physical layout of the building. Is it open and visible, or are there lots of little nooks and crannies? Is the bathroom/changing room visible? Is it possible for kids to hide away, or be hidden? My rule of thumb is that the more open-plan the building is, the better. If everyone can see what everyone else is doing, then that has to be a good thing.

➤ How are members of staff checked?

I always ask about background checks of staff. Background checks are no guarantee of safety, but at least it's something. There is also the obvious thing of checking on the qualifications of staff. My rule of thumb is that the more qualified preschool teachers you have, the better. People in training are also very good, because when you're a student you tend to take the whole thing very seriously and work very hard.

➤ What do they feed the kids?

This seems a bit obvious, but it's worth noting. Ask what the kids get for morning tea and afternoon tea. The more sugary crap they give kids, the less I like the place. I'm no food Nazi, but I'm not a big fan of sugary crap. While I don't really subscribe to the view that sugar makes all kids psycho, I do think lots of sugar is really bad for their teeth and also makes them fat. A look around the kitchen area will usually tell you a lot. Is there evidence that providing healthy food is a priority?

Another issue is what they give the kids to drink. Water or milk is good. Fruit juice is bad.

➤ What is the discipline policy?
Again, this is stuff you just ask. Find out how they manage kids' behaviour. Ask them what they would do if they had a kid who is a biter or a hitter. If their answers are confident and match up with the behaviour management principles we've talked about in earlier chapters, then this is good. You have to bear in mind, though, that daycare centres are not allowed to put kids in time out, since they have to be with staff at all time. (It seems barking mad to me that preschool teachers aren't allowed to put kids in time out, but that's just one more sign of the barking mad, nicey-nicey world we live in.)

➤ What are the information systems like?
What you're most interested in here is evidence of some logical, orderly system. While systems are no guarantee either — some places have great-looking systems but crap staff — at least you'll know there is a plan in place for getting you information about anything important that happens to your child.

➤ Spend some time observing the place
Most centres will let you come in a couple of times to inspect the place, and you should take advantage of that. The things you need to watch for include how they manage the children on a routine basis. Is it orderly and structured, without being anal? Do the kids get some direction from staff, or simply charge around in a big chaotic lump?

Also watch out for little incidents and see how the staff handle them. All little kids are periodically thug-like — it goes with the age — so if you wait long enough someone is bound to clout someone or shove someone. When that happens, see if anyone notices and what they do about it.

➤ What is the vibe?

This sounds a bit flouncy, but it's an important one: everything else aside, what is your gut feeling about the place? If you have any niggling doubts, listen to them. If the place feels warm, friendly, and child-focused, then all is good. If on the other hand it feels like a zoo, or emotionally cold, or the staff look as if they don't really want to be there, or you simply don't like it but you don't know why, then my advice is you're best to listen to that and keep looking until you find somewhere that feels right.

The babysitter issue

The world is a very PC place and it isn't really the done thing to make blanket statements about any particular group, whether it be on the basis of ethnicity, gender, sexual orientation, hair colour, or dental hygiene ('That's not bad breath, you bigot — it's oral diversity'). God forbid that we should offend someone, especially the orally diverse.

Of course the only problem with this is that there are people in the world who seem to have made it their life's work to be offended by anything they can. Often they will generously assume offence on behalf of others. I think the phrase *big girl's blouse* was probably coined for people like that.

While in my book *Into the Darklands* I didn't make any blanket statements about any of those groups, not even the orally diverse, I did say never have a teenage boy as a babysitter. This statement prompted one reviewer to remark that he thought I was paranoid and 'burnt out'. I think when I read that review my thought about him was that he was a prat.

So, even though some other reviewer will probably have a similar go at me, I will say it again: *never have a teenage boy as a babysitter.*

Am I saying all teenage boys are bad?

No.

Am I saying they are all perverts?

No.

Am I saying that your children are safer with teenage girls?

Yes, without doubt I am saying that.

I've worked with many teenage boys who have sexually offended against the children they were looking after. Some of these teenagers were good kids from good homes — they just made a very bad decision. I've worked with enough of these kids to convince me that I'd never have a teenage boy looking after my children. Because of that, I think it's fair enough I share this opinion with you so that you can make up your own mind.

Just for the record, though, do I think the young men of this nation give a monkeys about the fact that I've said this?

No.

Do I think that their fragile little self-esteems will be forever damaged because of what I've said?

No.

Teenage boys have much bigger issues going on than any comments I might make about babysitting.

I'll take a nice sensible teenage girl babysitter from a nice family over a nice sensible teenage boy babysitter from a nice family any day of the week.

You can do whatever seems best to you.

Fear is bad

The most important thing about keeping your kids safe is that you can't get too nutty about it. Fear is a natural part of parenting. Usually, the fear sets in even before conception, and lasts until you die. There are a gazillion bad things that can happen to kids, but most of them don't.

Despite the countless sharp objects that children seem drawn to play with over the course of their lives, most don't lose an eye. And even if they do, most still manage OK. My dad lost an eye when he was a kid when his cousin shot him with an arrow with a sucker on the end, yet still he managed to truck on and have a pretty good life.

Bad things happen — that is an unavoidable part of life — but good things happen, too.

Just like there were probably lots of kids today who broke an arm, or burnt their fingers, or lost an eye, there were countless more who probably laughed, played in the sun, got hugs, gave hugs, cried, sang, had dinner and went to bed.

Tomorrow they'll all get up and do it again.

You can't be ruled by fear, because that sucks the life out of life. Just be sensible, and hope nothing too bad comes your way.

That's all you can do.

22

How to stop your head
from exploding

If you're a parent, and you're actually present for any part of the day, you'll have strayed into that most dangerous of places: the point where you become so frustrated, angry, and generally exasperated that you actually feel like your head will explode. Not metaphorically explode, but *actually* explode in a shower of gore, teeth and bone. They never tell you about that place when you go to antenatal classes, or if they did you weren't listening, because it's always a surprise when you actually get there.

I remember about a month ago I became so angry, so enraged at the ridiculousness of the latest dispute between my two boys, that I actually had to go lie down. My head was pounding as the blood rushed about looking for somewhere to go. I could actually feel the arteries that supply vital parts of my brain creaking under the strain.

And what was it that caused all this? From memory, it was a completely insane dispute over an empty cardboard box that had been lying around largely ignored for the previous month. On that particular day, though, it was the most valued, the most prized possession in the entire world, and they both wanted it with the self-same passion with which Gollum wanted the Ring. There was shrieking, and demanding, and pleading, and shoving, and repeated blows thrown from one to the other. The utter ridiculousness of the dispute, and the length of time the whole thing went on, almost killed me.

We all end up in that place sooner or later, and sadly most of us will make large numbers of return trips over the years. We all get angry at our kids, and sometimes the anger is so intense we become slightly dizzy, and we hear a high-pitched ringing in our ears. If you don't go there from time to time, you're probably not spending enough time with the kids.

Having said all that, it's a dangerous place to be, because if you stay there too long it will take years off your life. So here are my top three tips for trying to go there less often, and for getting out quickly when you do. Much of this ties into dealing with really little people — because the preschool years can be pretty tumultuous as they struggle with issues of control and self-control — but much of what I'm going to say goes for bigger kids, too.

Get a plan

The big reason most parents feel enraged is because they feel powerless, because they're at the end of their proverbial tether, because nothing they've done has made any kind of difference up until that point. Most of us don't *want* to be angry — we just end up feeling that way because it's the last refuge of a sane mind. The utter helplessness of being ignored by tiny little people is inherently enraging. So you need to get a plan.

The plan doesn't have to be complicated. In fact, the best plans are the simplest ones. Just figure out where things start going pear-shaped, figure out what the little person is getting out of behaving in that way, and then figure out how you can make them think again. You might distract them, you might remind them that if they do what you want they get a sticker on their chart, you might tell them that if they keep doing what they're doing they will end up in time out, or any one of a number of things. It doesn't necessarily matter what you do, so long as you do something. If you have a plan you'll feel like you're in charge, and that will have magical calming qualities. If you don't have a plan you'll just react — and generally when we react to stuff we react emotionally, and generally that emotion is anger.

Keep it all in context

Sometimes it's very easy to begin to believe that your children actually want to kill you. It can be deceptively easy to give in to those dark thoughts and start believing they spend their days and nights scheming ways to drive you insane, and thereby kill you from sheer exasperation. This is hardly ever the case, though. In fact, I've never come across a toddler who wanted to kill their mum or dad.

The problem is that children have an exasperating tendency to act like . . . well . . . children. You have to keep reminding yourself that they've not been on the planet for long, and they've an enormous amount to learn. Just getting their heads around walking, talking and bowel control is quite a lot to do before you're five, let alone sorting out the pros and cons of good behaviour, and learning how to be responsible members of the household. Some adults are still struggling with that stuff.

So always keep in mind that they haven't been here very long, and that their little brains are only just beginning to wrap themselves around the world. You can't really expect them to show a huge amount of maturity and wisdom. If you expect pettiness and silliness, you'll be far less disappointed. To remind myself of this very important point, I have a conversation I often revisit with my boys when I feel in danger of forgetting it:

'Why do you always act like a six-year-old?' I say to my younger son.

'Because I am six,' he replies, slightly indignant.
'Ohhhh, yeah.'

Remember that life is suffering

This is back to the Buddhist thing we looked at in Chapter 7. Essentially Buddha said, some 2,500 years ago, that we often make ourselves unhappy because we expect that life should be comfortable, and easy, and generally better than it usually is. The problem is, of course, that life is imperfect, and it often contains long stretches of unpleasantness. This is doubly true of parenting. It's fantastic, and amazing, and the greatest adventure you will ever have — but sometimes it also really sucks. It's sometimes boring, and frustrating, and generally stressful.

And those are just the good days.

If you expect the process of raising kids to be this grand sparkling adventure all the time, you'll feel a bit let down. That will lead to feeling bitter, and then getting grumpy, and then getting angry, and then your head will explode and you'll die.

If you understand that we all experience these patches of grinding boredom, stress, frustration, and general misgivings, it makes the whole thing somehow easier to bear. If you stop struggling against the current — all the time trying to make your family life something it can never be (or at least something it can only be for brief, fleeting, wonderful moments) — then you can relax a little and deal with life as it is. Live where you are is my advice, not in some *Brady-Bunch*-like fantasy. None of us has it easy; that's simply part of the price you have to pay if you want to go on the ride. Once you get your head around that, the journey becomes considerably easier. Just to be on the safe side, though, it does pay to make sure the life insurance is all paid up.

It's always important to have a Plan B.

Putting it all together

So now you've got all the basic tools I use when I'm working with a family. The things we've talked about so far are my equivalent of hammers and nails. These are the bits and pieces I use to get the job done, be it the psychological equivalent of adjusting a door that won't close, or a major renovation that takes months longer than you expected and comes in way over budget.

The thing about many parenting books is that you're often left with a lot of good messages, but no real sense of what you actually do to pull all the different pieces into a coherent whole. This final section is my attempt at doing that.

As a result, first I'm going to give you a simple user's guide to this particular toolbox, because if you have a bunch of things going on you need a way to prioritize where to start and what to do. Then, as a graduation test, I'm going to introduce you to the Humdinger family, and let you practise your family-fixing skills on them.

They're nice people the Humdingers, but they've got a fair bit of stuff going on.

23

The toolbox:
a user's guide

By now I've given you a range of techniques to deal with problems with sleeping, eating, toilet-training, and behaviour. Use them as prescribed and they *will* work. I've also talked about some ways to teach kids skills to help them deal with problems such as shyness and low self-esteem.

Now I'm going to give you a way to organize all that into a coherent battle plan. If you have a bunch of different things going on, you need to know where to start and what to do from beginning to end.

Here's how you do that.

Triage

Just like rescue workers at a disaster scene, parents need a way to quickly assess the scale of the problem, and decide which area to start cleaning up first. My advice to parents who have a whole lot of different problems going on is that the first place you should start is a two-pronged attack on sleep and behaviour.

Sleep-deprived children are horrible, just horrible, so starting with that will shift things along quite quickly. As we saw earlier, sleep problems are also fairly easy to fix, so that will also help you feel more confident. If the kids are asleep earlier, that's also going to give you more 'big people time' at night once the children are tucked up. Big people time is very important if you are to stay sane over the long haul.

Of course, the next issue is which behaviours do you focus on first? The rule of thumb you use to make that decision is simple: *What bit of this currently drives me the craziest?*

Whatever answer comes out the end of that question will dictate where you start and what you do. If you are currently having problems across the board with almost everything, then simply pick the thing that makes you the craziest and start there — if it's kids constantly yelling inside the house, kids biting, meal times, or bad behaviour when you're out shopping, start there.

It doesn't really matter where you start, just so long as you *start*. Sitting in a corner, rocking quietly as the world comes down around your ears will not help. Getting up and getting going will.

The reason you make reducing your feelings of craziness the driving force is also simple: the crazier you are, the crazier they will be. Conversely, the saner you are, the saner they will be. Pick the thing that will make you feel the best the fastest.

So, focused triage is the key. Attend to any sleep problems first, then ask yourself which behaviours drive you the craziest, and start there. We'll talk about how you actually start next.

The kitset family fixer

This is the kitset version of what I do with the families I work with — the whole thing boxed up and ready to assemble at your place. Remember back at the very beginning I said that one of the most important rules was that you must, must, must have a plan? Well, here's a plan-making kit. I'm going to outline a simple five-step process you can use to tackle almost any kind of problem you might come across.

The Kitset Family Fixer

1 Clearly define the problem.

2 What is the behaviour saying?

3 What keeps the behaviour going?

4 Clearly define the goal.

5 Identify the steps and tools.

The nice thing about this kitset is that the instructions are really easy to understand, and there are no confusing diagrams. Just like all kitsets, though, you need to assemble the pieces one at a time. So follow the steps in an orderly fashion, and it will all be worth it in the end.

Step 1: Clearly define the problem

The trick here, as I've mentioned earlier, is to be specific in your descriptions. Write a description as if you're doing it for someone who doesn't know your child. This will force you to itemize the particular behaviours involved.

For example, 'grumpy after school' is a lot less useful than 'within 30 minutes of coming home from school will become non-compliant, saying "No", lying on the couch or floor watching television, refusing to answer when spoken to, on repeated requests becomes angry and throws objects or hits people'.

Step 2: What is the behaviour saying?

This is a crucial step, and one not to be rushed. If you get this right, the rest will be easy. If you get it wrong, your plan will fail. It's fine to get this wrong, so long as you realize this fairly smartly and come back and repeat this step until you get it right.

The biggest trap here is that it's easy, particularly if the behaviour is causing you some stress, to find a negative explanation: 'The reason Jenny gets out of bed at night and cries is that she doesn't like me very much and wants to ruin my evening.' That may be what you *feel*, but it's probably not the child's intention. For this reason use only positive terms and structure it *from the child's point of view* with a phrase that includes either 'I feel . . .' or 'I need . . .' For example: 'I get out of bed because I feel scared of the dark and want Mum and Dad to make me feel safe again'.

The reason for using 'I' statements and putting it in a more positive frame is that you are more likely to get a more accurate idea of what they are trying to say. Children are simple creatures at one level, with very simple needs. While it can sometimes feel as if they're doing things out of spite, mostly they're not. Mostly they just want very simple things.

Once you have a better idea of what they're trying to say with their behaviour, you'll have a better idea what they really need, and so you'll be better able to help them meet that need in a more positive way.

Step 3: What keeps the behaviour going?

For any behaviour to continue, there must be some kind of payoff. If you keep doing something and you get absolutely nothing for the effort, you'll eventually stop. This is true for any kind of behaviour — big people's and little people's.

Brutal honesty is called for here. You must take a long, hard look at what you are doing that may involve some kind of payoff for your little person. If you yell and scream all the time, the payoff is attention — noisy and unpleasant, but attention just the same. If you buckle to avoid a fight, the payoff is a sense of control. If you disagree with your partner in front of the child, the payoff is also control. If you constantly negotiate, the payoff is attention *and* control.

In general, the payoff will always be that the little person either gets something they want, or avoids something they don't want. All you need to do is figure out how the bad behaviour is helping them do that.

Step 4: Identify the goal

Again, fairly obviously, being specific is the key here. 'Being good at school' is not a goal. This is too broad, and so isn't very helpful. A better goal would be: 'Working hard at school all day doing what the teacher asks and not having to go in time out once during class.' This goal gives you something you can clearly evaluate. If the child gets through a day completing all tasks asked by the teacher, and does not go in time out, then we all get to party hard because we know the goal has been reached.

Step 5: Identify the steps and tools

As with the model for teaching skills I was talking about earlier, you want to break the goal down into bite-sized chunks. Sometimes 'being good' is too big a step, so you need to chop it up until the steps are the right size for little feet. This means that if the goal is 'going to bed by 7.00 p.m. without a fuss', then you break that down into steps:

Bath by 5.30 p.m.
Out and changed by 6.00 p.m.
Dinner by 6.30 p.m.
Story over by 6.50 p.m.
Teeth brushed by 6.55 p.m.
In bed by 7.00 p.m.
All steps achieved calmly and quietly, no yelling.

As soon as you see a series of steps such as this, it starts to suggest which of the various tools we've talked about are relevant. For younger children, for instance, the initial stages require a combination of directed attention reinforced with sticker charts, using distraction as much as possible, and then moving into the sleep programme tools from Chapters 6 to 9.

If you break everything down into steps, even time-based steps as in the above example, you are more likely to be able to anticipate problems and have some strategies up your sleeve to deal with them.

As with anything, you can even break the steps down into sub-steps. For example, if the little person in the above example gets themselves really worked up over baths, which then flows on into the rest of the evening, then you can use the process outlined in Chapter 5 for teaching new skills. This might involve some directed play where you bath Teddy, or watching a bigger sibling have a bath to see how they make it fun, or making up a story about the little girl who was afraid of losing her dirt.

The key concept here is to take your goal, break it down, and then use whatever tools you need to help you get there. See chart opposite.

In addition to this, we have also dealt with sleep and settling problems in Chapters 6 to 9, eating problems in Chapters 10 to 12, toilet-training in Chapters 13 and 14, and communicating with children in Chapters 15 to 17.

Be single-minded

Once you have triaged the behaviours, developed a plan, and moved into action using whichever tools seem the most appropriate, you must be single-minded in your pursuit of victory. As with Sleep Voodoo, there can be only one outcome here.

Ask, tell, do.

You might re-evaluate, but you will *not* go back. If they scream and cry, you will not buckle. If they beg and plead, you will not break.

Ask, tell, do.

Technique	Page ref	Ages	Problem level*	Key strengths
Directed attention	167–170	18 mths +	Low–med	Directly feeds good behaviours and starves bad ones.
Redirection	173–175	12 mths +	Low–med	Excellent way to avoid 90% of conflicts that might otherwise escalate.
Sticker charts	185–188	3.5–4 yrs	Low–high	Provides structure and leverage to turn negative behaviours back into positive ones.
Time out	190–195	3 yrs +	High	Effective way to extinguish bad behaviours.
Skills training	53–58	4 yrs +	Low–high	Good to teach the skills children need to prevent development of further difficulties.
Ladder of Certain Doom	205–211	6 yrs +	Med–high	Combines benefits of sticker charts and time out, and also removes negative emotion and fighting.

* Low-level problem behaviours: niggling, whining, minor tantrums.
   Medium-level problem behaviours: more persistent niggling, rough with toys or things, rude voice, non-compliance.
   High-level problem behaviours: hitting, disrespect, major tantrums, and continued non-compliance.

Your job as a parent is to be a dictator — a benign and compassionate one for sure, but a dictator nonetheless. Families do not work when they are run by committee with consumer representation in the decision-making.

Ask, tell, do.

They may say they hate you, but you don't have to listen. They may look heartbroken, but children's hearts are fairly robust. The simple act of being sent to bed early, for instance, will not usually break a child's heart. Neither will getting a sad face on their sticker chart.

Ask nicely.

Tell firmly.

And then, by golly, you *do*.

24

Flying solo:
the Humdinger family

NEW REFERRAL

Family details	Harry (35) and Sally (37), Crystal (9), Darnell (8), Darius (8), and Jed (4)
Presenting problem	This family is a creeping disaster. They all live in a two-bedroom rented house. Social workers have been threatening to remove the children because of the state of the house, and the way the parents treat the children. Both Harry and Sally acknowledge they smack the kids, and the neighbours regularly complain about the noise from all the yelling. The older children are often absent from school, and when they do go their behaviour is terrible. The twins, Darnell and Darius (8), have been getting in fights with other children at school, and their language is atrocious. Crystal (9) has difficulty making friends, and also swears and is aggressive. Jed (4) has been stood down from

	preschool for biting. He is not toilet-trained. Harry and Sally say that the children constantly fight, will not listen to anything they say, and do not sleep sometimes until almost midnight.
Notes	Holy dysfunction, Batman!

I've saved the 'worst' one for last, and this one you're going to solve all by yourself. By now you've got all the basic principles and tools to fix any problem, so I'm going to outline the case for you, and you can come up with your own plan. This is a real case, just by the bye — everything in here is how it really was.

In the next chapter, I've given you my analysis and the plan that I worked out with the family, but have a crack at it yourself first before you read that.

People like the Humdingers turned up everywhere I've ever worked. This family has so many problems that, in the staff meetings where new referrals are allocated, most people sit and stare at the floor so they don't get asked to pick up the case. There are so many problems in the Humdinger family that it's hard to know where to start. For some strange reason, I've always felt an overriding urge to put up my hand for these ones. Whenever they asked 'Who wants this one?', my hand somehow managed to find its way free and make the long haul up to volunteering altitude. 'Uh, I'll take it.'

It doesn't feel so scary now to go out and see the Humdingers, but in the beginning when I was just a student, and therefore knew very little, it was terrifying. I specialize in the Humdingers now, and I've met the entire Humdinger clan from one end of the country to the other. This is a big family, with little Humdinger offshoots pretty much everywhere. There will undoubtedly be a local Humdinger branch in your town. The Humdingers are not bad people, not once you get to really know them — they're just struggling a bit more than the rest of us. All they need is a bit of help to put the wheels back on.

So in that spirit, I hereby allocate the Humdingers to you. This is as good a place as any to start. There's a lot going on for these guys, as you're about to find out, and you're going to have to think quite hard about how you're going to help them. But help them you will, because you're all they've got.

Besides, it's best to practise on someone else's kids first. I practised for 10 years before I had a go at raising my own. My advice would be that the best place to start is with a home visit.

The home visit

As soon as you drive up, you can see that this is not a *Better Homes and Gardens* home. In fact, it looks more like a *Derelict Homes and Gardens* home. The front door is ajar, despite the fact that it's quite cold, and it's really only half a door — the bottom half is planks of wood nailed over holes that have obviously been kicked in at some time.

A small dog sits on the front step watching you. Even the dog is odd-looking, as if it came from the seconds bin at a dog-making factory. Its head seems just a little too big for such a tiny body. As you approach, it starts to shake and growl, although it is such a tiny neurotic thing it's hard to know if it is in a rage or terrified. The point becomes moot anyway, as it turns tail and vanishes inside.

As you approach the door, you hear the sound of electronic gunshots from inside, and you notice that one of the windows has been broken and fixed with a piece of cardboard taped to the window. A single small blue Wiggles gumboot lies heartbroken on the stoop, pining for its mate.

You reach up: knock, knock, knock.

'Get the door,' a man says from somewhere inside.

'No.' A boy's voice, snarky.

'Do as your father says.' This time a woman.

'*No*, it's my turn now.'

'No, it isn't,' a girl snaps. 'It's mine.'

'*No, it isn't*,' the first boy squeals.

'*Darnell*, will you *get* the *bloody door*!' bellows the man.

'*No*.'

'*Darnell*—'

'*NO! FUCK OFF!*' There is a stomping of small feet, presumably Darnell's, and then a door slams so hard that the broken window beside you rattles.

'Jesus Christ, what the hell is wrong with that boy?'

Silence, apart from the electronic gunshots.

You stand there for a few moments, unsure what to do. Once it's obvious that they've forgotten the door, you knock again.

'Will you get the door, Bubba?'

Whatever happens next, you tell yourself, whatever comes out of there, you must not scream.

And then the first Humdinger appears, little Jed, aged four. He's wearing dirty jeans and a pyjama top. He looks up at you with a frown.

'Who is it, Bubba?' a woman calls out from inside.

Jed — who apparently also works under the alias Bubba — looks up at you, all frowns and dirty face. 'Man,' he finally calls out, not even dinting the frown.

The woman's voice, quieter this time: 'Did you pay the washing-machine people?'

The man: 'Yeah.'

'Are you sure?'

'Course I'm bloody sure.'

A squeak of couch springs and the sound of approaching scuffing feet.

Momma Humdinger cometh, you think to yourself.

And then suddenly there she is: Sally Humdinger, looking suspicious. 'Yes?'

'Hi,' you say, trying to sound cheery and telling her your name, 'I'm from Family Fixers.'

'Family what?' Sally asks, and you see where Jed gets his frown.

'Family Fixers,' you say, and add the tagline from your advertisement on the telly: 'No family too big or too small.'

Sally just looks at you blankly. 'You're not here about the washing-machine payment?'

You shake your head. 'No, I've come to help you and Harry with the kids.'

Suddenly a light goes on and Sally looks excited: 'Are you like that Super Nanny on the telly?'

You sigh. 'Kind of, except she's really annoying and I'm not.'

Sally laughs, and when she does she looks much younger. 'Come in, come in.'

The scene inside is pretty much like outside, just with less grass and sky, and more kids. The family is gathered around the television with the curtains pulled to keep the light down. They are engaged in a family session of what appears to be an incredibly violent video game.

As you walk in, Darius shoots two policemen who collapse in a splatter of blood. Crystal sits on the arm of the sofa next to her dad. She is still in her school uniform, which makes her look oddly normal in the swirling chaos that is the Humdinger house. Harry is sprawled out on the couch, smoking, and watching his eight-year-old son shoot cops.

'Harry, this is the person who's come to talk to us about the kids.'

The neurotic little dog, who you will come to know — and loathe — as Gollum, sits shaking under the sofa.

Harry pulls himself to his feet as you walk in. He extends a hand, and as he does you take in the unshaven face and nicotine-stained teeth. Harry's wearing track pants and woollen socks with a black T-shirt that seems to be trying to make the point that if you drink a particular brand of bourbon you'll be rugged and cool.

Harry is certainly rugged, although not necessarily in a good way.

From the corner of your eye as you are introducing yourself to Harry you notice Bubba Frown poking Darius, who ignores him for a second, then suddenly explodes and shoves little Bubba so hard he falls over and hits his head on the ground, promptly breaking out into an aggrieved howl.

'*Darius!*' barks Harry, whirling around at the boy. '*Get to your room!*'

'*But he—*'

'*Just get OUT.*'

Darius throws the PlayStation controller to the ground and storms out the front door.

'That boy drives me crazy,' says Harry, watching his son disappear outside. 'He doesn't listen to a thing we say.'

Crystal swoops in meanwhile and grabs the controller. Bubba Frown scrambles to his feet and starts to poke her. Sally watches it all and says nothing. Actually, you think her eyes look kind of glazed, tinted with the resignation of the truly damned.

'Shall we go in the kitchen to talk?' you ask.

Actually, the kitchen is a pleasant surprise. It is clean and orderly, with a bowl of fruit on the table. The kids' drawings are up on the fridge. If it wasn't for the fact that in the back corner you can see the long-lost mate of the blue Wiggles gumboot from the front door, this could be like any other kitchen.

'OK,' you say, sounding confident. 'Tell me about the problems you're having.'

And they do.

All of this with a backdrop of yelling, screaming, and thudding, from the living room next door. It sounds like a serial-killer Christmas party is going on in there, but you bravely ignore it as you listen to Harry and Sally talk.

It turns out that there are not many problems they don't have. Jed isn't toilet-trained yet, which places extra financial strain on the family, given that nappies aren't cheap. In addition, he has a real problem with biting — Sally shows you the teeth marks to prove it.

'What do you do when he bites?' you ask.

'Bite him back,' she says. 'It's the only way to get the message through to him.' Judging by the bite marks, he isn't getting that message terribly clearly.

Jed, or Bubba Frown, appears to have a general problem with aggression. In addition to biting, he also hits and uses foul language at preschool. He's on the verge of being expelled, and he's not even five years old.

None of the children sleep well. In fact, they hardly sleep at all. At least part of the reason for this is apparent when you have a look in their room. There is a television in one corner on a scarred dresser. All four kids sleep in the same room in two sets of bunks. Because it takes so long for them all to go to sleep — usually the last one is off around midnight — Harry and Sally put them all to bed at the same time, usually sometime around 6 p.m. is when the circus starts each night. Juice, television, crying, yelling. Just about every bad bedtime thing.

The children fight constantly with each other. Crystal is the oldest, and you think she's the smartest after having watched them all together for a while. She tends to sit back and pull the strings, winding everyone else up. Darnell appears to be the most explosive of the bunch, something that Bubba Frown seems to enjoy. Although when you watch them closely, Bubba Frown seems to be provoking the older boys more to get sympathy from his parents than because he likes being hit.

School is a disaster. The boys are in constant trouble with their teacher, and have recently been put in separate classes. They didn't like this but have settled slightly. They are falling behind in their schoolwork, and seem determined to be the roughest kids at school. Darius, the quieter of the two boys, has begun bullying younger kids at school.

Crystal is doing OK with her schoolwork, and isn't causing any problems for her teacher, but appears to have major difficulties making friends. Her teacher says she is isolated from the other girls and doesn't seem interested in forming friendships. Your impression is that she seems kind of angry and shut down, but no one seems to notice, or at least not that you can see anyway.

When you ask Harry and Sally to describe the daily routine, they look at you blankly.

'You know,' you say. 'Describe a typical day.'

Harry shrugs. 'They just get up and start fighting, then that lasts all day, then they go to bed.'

'What have you tried?' you ask them.

'Everything,' says Sally.

'Such as?'

She sighs: 'Everything. We've used star charts, and time out, yelling, smacking — everything.'

'Has any of that worked?'

'Smacking is about the only thing they take any notice of,' says Harry.

You reflect back on the interactions you've seen, and so far as you can recall you haven't seen a single positive interaction between the children and their parents. Not one.

'And how are the two of you doing?' you ask as you get to the end of the interview. Sally bursts into tears, and Harry puts an arm around her shoulder. 'It's pretty hard,' he says.

And you can hear it in his voice, the thin edge of desperation.

Sitting there watching them, you understand that these two really do love their kids, it's just that things have gotten way out of hand.

'Right,' you say, sitting up straighter and using your *don't-worry-I-know-what-I'm-doing* voice, 'shall we fix all this up for you guys?'

Harry nods. Sally sniffs, wiping her eyes and looking up at you. Then you open your mouth, and begin to speak . . .

OK, so where is it going pear-shaped?

The first thing you have to do is work out where you think it's all going wrong. There are a lot of issues here, so you're going to need to come up with something that can take account of all that.

My suggestion would be to go back to the rules I outlined in Chapter 1 and see which ones you think are being ignored or violated. This will help you figure out where to start.

❖ Remember the three Rs

❖ Loving is easy, liking is hard

❖ Children are piranhas

❖ Feed the good, starve the bad

❖ Kids need fences

❖ Be consistent-ish

❖ Don't take any crap

❖ You gotta have a plan

❖ All behaviour is communication

❖ Embrace chaos

Triage

There's a lot going on here, so much so that even a lot of professionals can get a bit lost. It's easy to lose your way in the fog. The trick is to focus on simple things, focus on where the heat is — where you can get the most traction. I've talked about some ways to get started in the previous chapter.

What you'll need to do here is write down a simple list of

10 points, itemizing which things you'd begin with, and where you'd go next. Don't worry about writing out some big plan — just write out your 10 bullet points, and check them against the ones that I ended up developing with Harry and Sally. I'll give you our answers in the next chapter, but for now you have a crack and see what you come up with.

At this point everything is up for grabs: if you walked into that house, where would you start? You could think that fixing the front door was the most important place to start, or you could think that it was turning off the television. The first move is up to you. Then what would you do next? What would you do after that . . . all the way to number 10.

Tools

Once you have your simple 10-step list, I want you to add in the tools you'd use for each step. Again, life is short so don't write an essay — just string a line off each step and write the name of the tool you'd use.

Some of this is complicated because we've predominantly talked about these things in relation to the home, but the Humdinger kids have problems outside of home as well. Do you think you can use these techniques in school? How would you do that? What would you suggest to Harry and Sally?

Remember, this stuff is all about basic principles, and basic principles apply everywhere. You might have to adjust things a little to fit the Humdingers. This is good practice because every kid is different, both yours and the Humdingers. You're never going to get the perfect paint-by-numbers solution.

Adapt or perish, that's the concept you have to grasp if you're going to survive the parenting game.

Once you've done all that, flip the page and see how your answers and mine compare. But no peeking first, because cheats never prosper. Well, hardly ever.

25

Ten steps to Humdinger happiness

First off, I hope you haven't cheated and skipped ahead to look at this without first having a go yourself. If you do have a list, then well done. These are the 10 steps I developed with Harry and Sally, and the order in which we tackled them. See how our plan stacks up against yours.

1 Clean up the place

You can't get a family in order if everyone lives in a chaotic mess, so cleaning up is an essential first step.

♣ Tidy up the mess inside and out.

♣ No smoking inside.

♣ Get rid of all the violent computer games.

♣ Harry has to shave every day, and both parents need to get themselves tidy and clean. You have to look the part if you want to act it.

2 Sort out the sleeping issues

Sleep deprivation will undoubtedly be making things worse.

♣ Get rid of the television from the kids' room.

♣ No juice at night.

✤ Establish a good bedtime routine for *all* of the kids, taking account of different ages.

✤ Stagger the children so Jed goes first at 7.00 p.m., then the twins at 8.00 p.m., then Crystal at 8.30 p.m.

✤ Because there is only one room, Jed can settle to sleep in his parents' room and then be moved back to his own bed once everyone else is asleep. Use Sleep Voodoo with the little guy. Obviously this isn't ideal, but sometimes you have to make do. As his settling to sleep improves, he can be moved back into his own room in time.

✤ The three older kids can be rewarded with extra time on PlayStation for good settling, and lose 15-minute blocks for disturbing others. Harry and Sally are to be ruthless about taking away time for disturbing others.

3 Establish the basics

✤ Basic routine for the day including times for some kind of family activity (going out for a walk or playing a board game).

✤ Rules of the home (five maximum and written on a piece of paper stuck on the fridge). Should include things like no violence, talking respectfully, helping when asked etc.

4 Put behaviour management plan in place

✤ Clearly identify high-, medium- and low-level problem behaviours.

✤ Use a sticker chart for Jed, with time out for high-level problem behaviours (such as biting, hitting, and swearing).

✤ Focus on positive behaviours using directed attention.

✤ Strong focus on redirection.

❖ Use the 1-2-3 count and the microwave timer.

❖ Use a modified Ladder of Certain Doom for older kids. Instead of going to bed early (because there's only one room for all the kids) use time on PlayStation.

5 Focus on building more positive relationship between the children and their parents

❖ Directed attention and increased use of praise will help.

❖ Make spending structured positive time with kids a priority (such as going for walks to the skateboard park with the boys and telling them how good they are).

❖ Keep a simple diary of this so we can review this.

6 Meet with preschool to discuss Jed's behaviour and work out management strategy

❖ Ideally the preschool and home will do the same things (praise the same good behaviours and ignore/punish the same bad behaviours).

7 Meet with the three older children's teachers

We need to be clear about exactly what's happening at school, and to come up with a plan to manage the bad behaviours.

❖ The same tools can be used at school to triage and work out where to start.

❖ Much of the school behaviour stuff will be tied in to getting home more settled, better sleep, and developing a more positive relationship between the children and their parents.

❖ Sticker charts can flow backwards and forwards between school, as can the targets for the directed attention.

❖ If the behaviour at school escalates to an unacceptable point, Harry and Sally are to go and get the offending child, bring them home, and place them in time out in their room, with nothing to do until the end of school. When this happens, there will be no PlayStation or any other kind of treat.

❖ The main thing is to work with the classroom teachers as a team to solve the problem using the tools we've already talked about.

8 Use the rewiring process from Chapter 5 to teach the children new social skills and help them to make and keep friends

9 Focus on Harry getting a job

❖ This family desperately needs some financial stability. Money doesn't solve everything, but it does help most things.

❖ If Harry is working, this will also bring another level of structure into the house.

❖ Money will also mean Harry and Sally can do some things for themselves.

10 Last, and least, toilet-train Jed

❖ Use the toilet-training programme from Chapter 13.

❖ No point even going there with toilet-training until all the other stuff is more under control.

Now, I'm not saying that there is only one way to do this, or that this plan is even the best one. It's simply the plan that we used once we laid everything out on the table and started to sort through it all. There are a hundred different ways to do most things.

So how did you do with your plan?

Obviously this is a bit of a long haul, because some of the things on this list are going to take a while. In fact, if you look at the list it looks a bit like a full-time job. The reason for this is because *it is*. If you're at the bottom of a big hole — and the Humdingers were — you don't get out overnight, or by devoting a couple of hours a week to fixing the problem.

There are some steps that we put into place almost immediately, such as tidying up, the sleep programme, and the behaviour stuff. Other things, such as Harry's job and working on the issues at school, unfolded over several months.

The trick is simply to gain some focus, and get some momentum. Once you're moving, you commit to the end. There's no leaving until the Humdingers are fixed.

To their credit, Harry and Sally worked damn hard, and six months later things were in a far healthier state. The house was tidier, they had a good bedtime routine, and the conflict had reduced by about 75%, which was pretty good. Crystal was doing much better at school and was making some friends. The boys still had their ups and downs, but generally they were on an upward swing more often than not.

And here's where I love this stuff, because just as we're all sitting around one afternoon reflecting on all the positive change and feeling good about what they'd achieved, Sally puts down her cup and says, 'There's just one thing, though.'

'What?' I asked.

'Where's Jed going to sleep when the new baby arrives?'

Bugger.

Driving home one night . . .

26

How the story ends

I'd like to say that this will all get easier with time, but it probably won't. I don't think it necessarily gets any harder either. It just changes. They'll master bowel control and then move on to boy control in little over a decade.

In truth I don't think it could get any harder or most of us probably *would* go mad — the barking kind with the tight-fitting overcoats that lace up at the back.

This job, this parenting thing, at times leaves you hanging on to your sanity in a white-knuckle grip. There'll be moments — and you've probably had them already — when you stand on the brink of madness, moments when you feel all rational thought falling away. There'll be tears along the way, all kinds of them.

Take what comfort there is to be had from the fact that we *all* have those white-knuckle moments, just as our parents did with us. I've been working for over 20 years with some of the most difficult kids you could ever hope to find — kids some people are afraid to even sit in the same room with — and still there are times when my own sweet boys make me feel as if my head is literally about to burst. The white-knuckle moments are just another part of the ride that either they didn't tell you about before you got on, or if they did you simply weren't listening.

Remember, too, that you don't have to be into all this modern hype and worry about every last little thing. You don't have to get all anxious and protective, and you don't have to solve every last little problem for them. Let them get dirty, let them climb trees, let them figure stuff out for themselves. There's nothing wrong with the odd bit of frustration, the odd graze, or even a fracture or two. At least if you let your kids get out there in the world and explore a bit, they've got a much better chance of having some decent scars to tell stories about later in life than the cage-reared young of the 'modern parent'.

It's also good to keep in mind that parenting is not a competitive sport. This might be hard at times, because often people around you will act as though it is — clucking madly over little Portia's stellar progress in violin, or proudly displaying Tarquin's global-warming class project that they did for him the night before.

Bollocks to all that nonsense.

Let your kids do what they enjoy — and if that's hitting a tree with a stick rather than playing Bach on the violin, then more power to them. Lots of great things probably began with some kid hitting a tree with a stick and thinking about stuff. Einstein didn't do 18 different after-school activities, and he still made his mark on the world.

You'll notice I haven't written about looking after yourself, or taking time with your partner (if they're still there) to keep your relationship young and fresh, and vital. Yeah, right.

Hang on to sanity as hard as you can — that's about all you can do. And so far as the relationship stuff goes, my only advice is this: as much as you can, be gentle with each other on the road. You have a long way to go yet.

A few months ago I was driving home one night and realized something so sad that it hit me like a punch. If we're lucky, none of us gets to see how the story ends for our children. It's simple, and kind of obvious, but I'd just never thought about it before.

Despite all the white-knuckle crap, when you're a parent you'd die for your kids without a second thought. Even on the worst days I would step into the fire for my boys without blinking.

There would be no hesitation or debate.

I want to be there for everything. I want to be there for every last little thing. I was there when they were born, for first steps, first words, first day at school, all that great stuff.

I want to be there for everything, but I know that isn't how it works. I won't get to see how it turns out for them. We might get to write the beginning of the story, but we don't get to write the end, just as our parents don't for us.

For this reason it's important to understand that this job we do — raising our kids — isn't just about eating dinner without a fight, or using manners, or getting through the day without going nuts. In the final analysis, it isn't really about any of those things. In the end, we are teaching them to write their own stories.

Our job isn't just to get through until bedtime; our job is to teach them how to *be*. One day they will travel on without us, and everything we do from the moment they hit the ground until the moment we leave it influences how they will do that.

We have to teach them to be good people.

We have to teach them to know right from wrong, and to *do* the right thing even when that's the *hardest* thing.

We have to teach them to fight for the things they believe in, and to speak out against that which they know to be wrong.

We have to teach them to look after the little guy, and to stand up to the bully.

We have to teach them how to strive to be all that they can be, and at the same time to be happy with who they are.

We have to teach them to be *proud*.

We have to teach them the value of connection.

Above all other things, we must teach them how to love, and be loved.

Somewhere up ahead of us all lies a blank page. That's the place where we put the pen down and our children pick it up. That's the place where they begin to write their own stories.

What will your children write?